HBJ Social Studies

PLACES WE KNOW

 Harcourt Brace Jovanovich, Inc.

Holt, Rinehart and Winston, Inc.

Orlando · Austin · San Diego · Chicago · Dallas · Toronto

SENIOR EDITORIAL ADVISER

Dr. Judith M. Finkelstein is the Associate Director of the Regents' Center for Early Developmental Education at the University of Northern Iowa, Cedar Falls, Iowa. Her Ph.D. in Early Childhood Curriculum was granted from the University of Minnesota. Dr. Finkelstein has taught at the Price Laboratory School developing social studies programs at the nursery/kindergarten and first-grade levels and has served as a consultant to numerous schools. Dr. Finkelstein has published widely in the area of early developmental education, as well as in *Social Education, The Social Studies*, and *Social Studies and the Young Learner*.

REVIEWERS

Joyce M. Buckner, Ed.D.
Director of Elementary Education
Omaha Public Schools
Omaha, Nebraska

Peggy A. Burgess
Teacher
Awbrey Park Elementary School
District 4 J
Eugene, Oregon

Jean Burke
Teacher
Webster School
Green Bay, Wisconsin

Estella M. Frantz
Teacher
Hinks Elementary School
Alpena, Michigan

Dorothy Macdonald
Director
Brown School
Schenectady, New York

Murry R. Nelson, Ph.D.
Professor of Education
Division of Curriculum and
   Instruction
The Pennsylvania State University
University Park, Pennsylvania

Sharon A. Pitts, Ed.D.
Principal
Meadows Elementary School
Terre Haute, Indiana

Cassie Wheelis
Teacher
Dartmouth Elementary School
Richardson, Texas

Judith S. Wooster, Ed.D.
SPICE Director
Stanford Program on International
   and Cross-Cultural Education
Stanford University
Stanford, California

CHILDREN'S LITERATURE ADVISER

Arlene F. Gallagher, Ph.D.
Adjunct Professor
Boston University
Boston, Massachusetts

ACKNOWLEDGMENTS

For permission to reprint copyrighted material, grateful acknowledgment is made to the following sources:

David A. Adler and Tumbledown Editions: From *A Little at a Time* by David A. Adler, illustrated by N. M. Bodecker. Text copyright © 1976 by David A. Adler; illustrations copyright © 1976 by N. M. Bodecker; illustrations copyright © 1989 by Tumbledown Editions. Color added to original illustrations with permission. Published by Random House, Inc.

Holt, Rinehart and Winston, Inc.: Music and lyrics from "Canoe Song," in *Holt Music*, Grade 3. Copyright © 1988 by Holt, Rinehart and Winston, Inc.

Houghton Mifflin Company: Text and illustrations from *How My Parents Learned to Eat* by Ina R. Friedman. Text copyright © 1984 by Ina R. Friedman; illustrations copyright © 1984 by Allen Say.

Viking Penguin, a division of Penguin Books USA Inc.: Text and illustrations from *Ox-Cart Man* by Donald Hall, illustrated by Barbara Cooney. Text copyright © 1979 by Donald Hall; illustrations copyright © 1979 by Barbara Cooney Porter.

Printed in the United States of America
ISBN 0-15-372527-3

CONTENTS

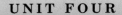

UNIT SIX
PLACES IN MY WORLD

187

Remembering Maps

This is a **map** of a school.
A map shows a place.
The place is seen from above.

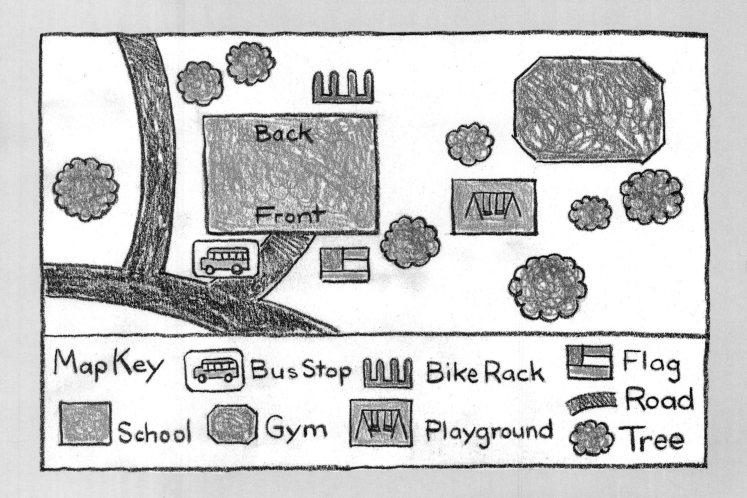

Most maps use **symbols.**
Symbols stand for real things.
A **map key** tells what the symbols mean.

This is another map of a school.
Look at the map and the map key.
What can you find on this map?
How is this map like the other map?
How is it different?

Map Key

Store

Tree

Park

School

House

Road

Here is another map.

Look at the map and the map key.
Then answer the questions.

1. What is in the middle of the map?

2. How many houses are there?

3. How many stores are there?

4. What is between the school and the houses?

5. What is behind the school?

6. Which road is in front of the school?

UNIT 1
Places and Changes

5

What is a neighborhood?

A **neighborhood** is a place where people live.

What could you tell someone about your neighborhood? You could start by telling about the things you see when you walk around your neighborhood.

Go with a boy and his grandfather as they take a walk in their city neighborhood.

A LITTLE
AT A TIME

By David A. Adler

Illustrated by N. M. Bodecker

How did that tree get to be so tall, Grandpa?
How did it get so tall?

When it started
it was just a seed.
Then it grew
and grew and grew and grew,
but it only grew
a little at a time.

And how come I'm so small?

When I was your age
I was smaller than you.
You'll grow,
not as tall as that tree,
but maybe taller than me.
You'll grow
the way I grew,
a little at a time.

Were the buildings here always this high, Grandpa?

Buildings here were much smaller
when I was your age.
But as more room was needed
small buildings were torn down,
and on the same land
higher buildings were built.
A city this big
is always changing
a little at a time.

Grandpa, why is this street so dirty?
How did it get like this?

Many people drop things.
Each person may drop
only a little,
but with so many people
dropping just a little,
this street became dirty
a little at a time.

How did this hole get to be so deep?
How did it get so deep?

Watch that steam shovel.
Each time the shovel drops down
and digs up some dirt,
the hole gets deeper.

But Grandpa,
the hole doesn't look any deeper.

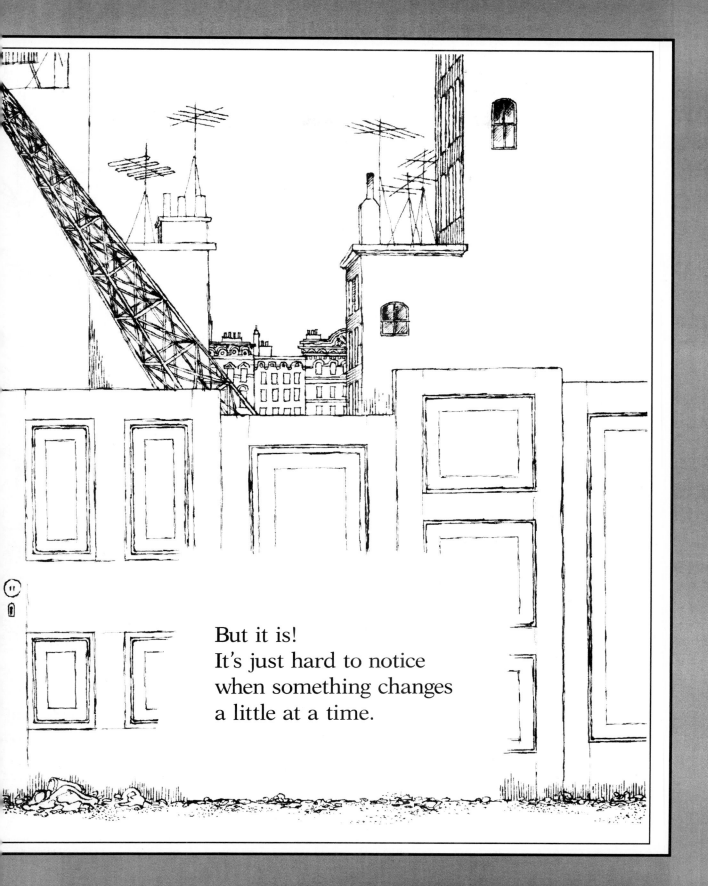

But it is!
It's just hard to notice
when something changes
a little at a time.

And the air, Grandpa,
it's so full of smoke.
Why?

Cars, buses, trucks, chimneys—
all give off smoke.
And with so many things
giving off a little smoke,
the air became dirty
the same as the streets—
a little at a time.

It's time now
to start going home,
but don't run ahead.
Your grandpa travels
just
a little at a time.

I think it's time for my nap now.

But how did it get so late, Grandpa?

You should know the answer to that!
The day is over
very quickly it seems,
but really it went by
just like everything else —
a little at a time.

What can I learn from this story?

Neighborhoods grow and **change** over time. Each neighborhood and the people who live there are special.

A group of neighborhoods forms a **community.** A city is a large community. A town is a small community.

Neighbors share things in their neighborhood. They share the trees, streets, and buildings. When there are problems, they share the problems, too.

Think About This

What could have changed this neighborhood?
What do you think the neighbors will do?

23

In the story, Grandpa lived in a city. Some people live in **suburbs.** Suburbs are communities near cities. Suburbs also have neighborhoods. This photograph shows a suburb from the air. What are some things you can see?

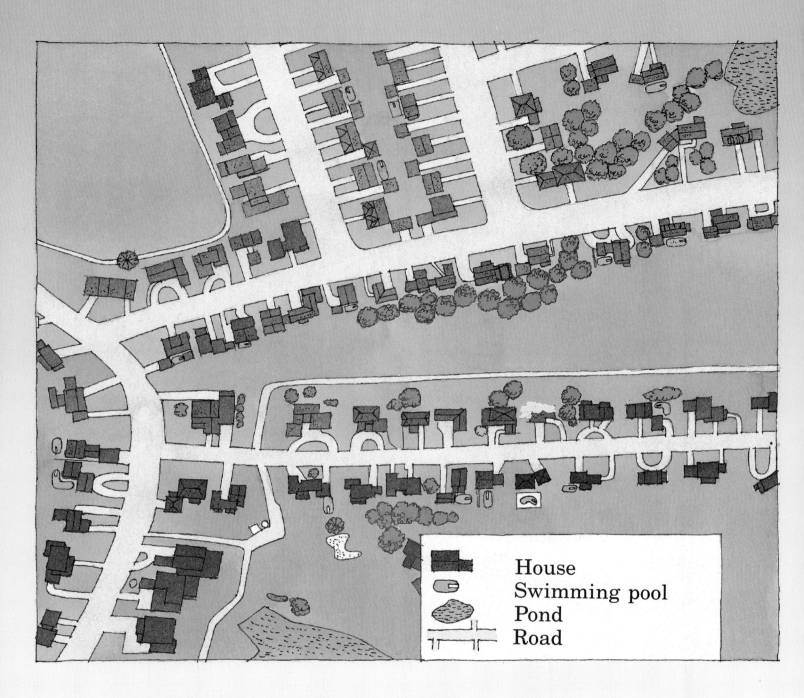

House
Swimming pool
Pond
Road

Here is a map of the same suburb.

1. How is the map like the photograph?
2. What things are in the photograph that are not on the map?
3. Can you find all the things on the map key?

**Ben Franklin's
Neighborhood**

Ben Franklin was a printer who lived long ago in the city of Philadelphia. Ben's print shop had paper, ink, and printing presses.

One day Ben said, "This neighborhood needs a book store." Soon he began selling books in his print shop.

"Now," Ben said, "this neighborhood needs a general store." He added shelves for pins and candles and feathers along with the books in the print shop.

Another day Ben said, "This neighborhood needs a post office." Ben set up a counter to handle the mail for the people of Philadelphia.

The city's leaders named Ben the Postmaster of Philadelphia.

Ben loved to read, but his print shop was too crowded for more books. Ben thought and thought. "I have it!" he exclaimed. "What this neighborhood needs is a library." So Ben raised money for a library. It was the first of its kind in America.

Then Ben asked, "Where can someone go to school in Philadelphia?" He organized a school and called it the Philadelphia Academy. It became the University of Pennsylvania.

Ben looked around and said, "This city needs a fire department." His fire department was the first in America.

Ben Franklin traveled far and wide. He became very famous. He wrote books and helped his country. He was a scientist and an inventor. Every day Ben looked around to see how he could make his neighborhood a better place.

Who is responsible for my neighborhood?

Neighbors are people who live near one another. Neighbors can work together to help solve problems. You and your neighbors can keep your neighborhood clean. You can recycle glass and paper. You can keep the parks beautiful. You can repair old buildings.

Neighbors can protect their neighborhoods for the future.

Think About This

How can cleaning up and recycling today help people in the future?

THE RECYCLING SONG

(Sung to the tune of "Ballin' the Jack.")

Separate your garbage, day and night,
Plastic on the left and aluminum on the right.
Bundle up old newspapers good and tight.
Then you flatten down some cardboard
with all of your might.

Save plastic bottles as a rule.
Gather up old phone books, don't be a fool.
They'll make new products, quick as a flash.
And that's what we call recycling trash!

**(from the students at Ventura Elementary School,
Orlando, Florida)**

Richmondtown

Richmondtown is a very old town. It is on Staten Island in New York. Richmondtown is one of the oldest towns in the United States. It began as a neighborhood where roads crossed.

In Richmondtown today, you can see old buildings. You can see where people lived. You can see where children went to school.

You can see people dressed in clothes from long ago.

In the old buildings you can see a pottery shop, a barrel-maker's shop, a carpenter's shop, and other shops, too. Most shops were a part of the shop owners' houses.

You could not move to Richmondtown, because no one lives there today. It is only a place to visit. It is kept just the way it was long ago. That way you can see what a neighborhood was like long ago in the United States.

Think About This

How is your neighborhood like this neighborhood from long ago? How is it different?

Garrett Morgan—The Man Who Changed Streets and Roads

In the year 1923 cars were a new form of transportation. As Garrett Morgan drove his new car through Cleveland, Ohio, he came to a cross street. He stopped at the corner. The traffic sign said STOP.

In those days there were no traffic lights. Traffic officers turned the signs from STOP to GO. Garrett waited and waited for the traffic officer to come and turn the sign to GO. The sign stayed on STOP. The line of waiting cars grew very long.

"There must be a better way to move traffic," Garrett thought as he sat.

"I've got it!" Garrett suddenly said out loud. "I'll make a new traffic sign. My new sign will turn halfway between STOP and GO. People will know when they see the sign turned halfway that they have to slow down and cross the street carefully. Then the traffic officer will not have to hurry back to change it."

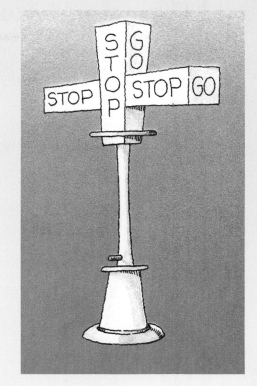

The yellow traffic lights we have today began with Garrett's invention. He changed his neighborhood for the better.

Think About This

How can people today help solve traffic problems?

How is my neighborhood like other neighborhoods in the world?

Neighborhoods all over the world are alike in many ways.

In many neighborhoods, there are places to shop and places for people to meet.

Neighborhoods are places where people go to school.

Neighborhoods are places where people have fun.

Think About This

How are these neighborhoods like the one where you live? How are they different?

The map on page 37 shows the neighborhood where Diana and Gabriel live. In the corner of the map is a **compass rose.** A compass rose shows the **directions** on a map. North, south, east, and west are directions. Directions tell which way to go.

Look at the map. Use the compass rose and the map key to answer the questions.

1. Is the hospital north or south of the library?

2. Is the school east or west of the hospital?

3. Diana walked from the park to the library. Did she walk east or west?

4. Gabriel lives on Third Street. He walked from his house to the park. Did he walk north or south?

5. Diana walked from the park to her house on Green Street. In which direction did she walk?

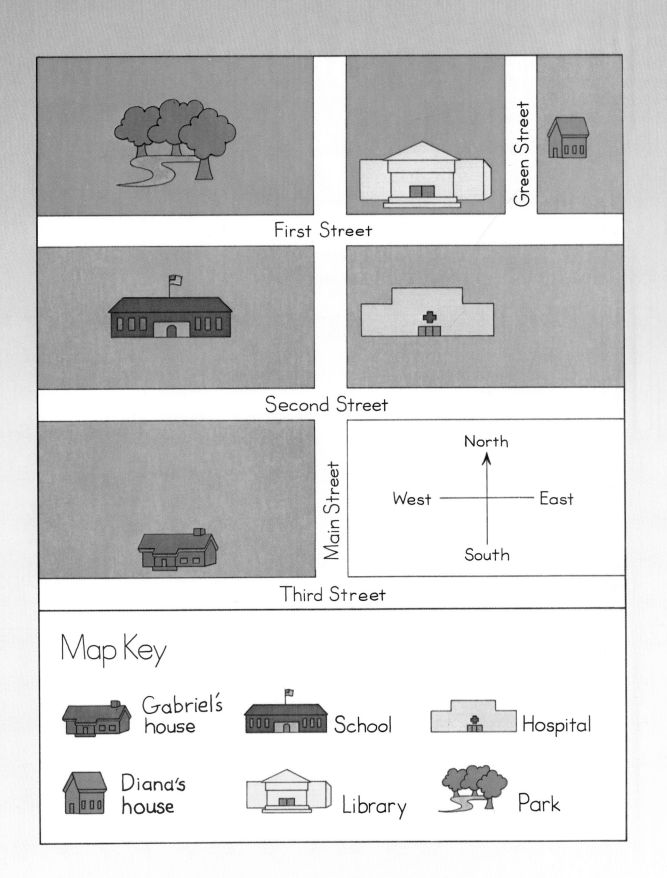

Skills in Action

Maps show more than where things are. They also show **distance.** Distance is how far one place is from another. One way to measure distance is by counting blocks.

This map shows José's neighborhood. José's address is 54 Bush Street. Find José's house on the map.

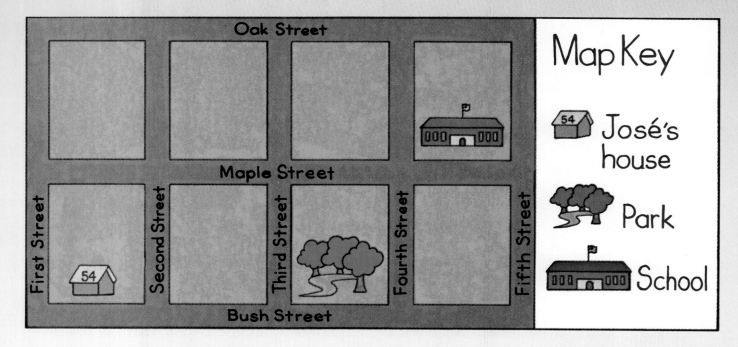

Use the map key to answer the questions.

1. How many blocks are there between José's house and the park?

2. How many blocks are there between José's house and the school?

Not all maps have blocks to count. Look at this map. Who lives closer to Lisa — Oscar or Sandra?

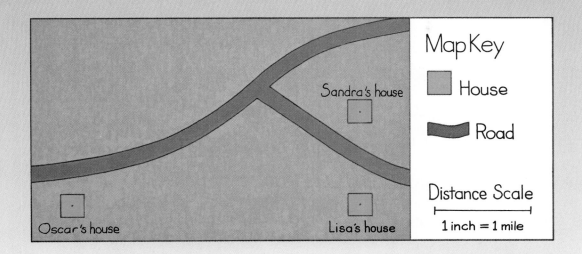

Suppose you want to know exactly how far each house is from Lisa's house. You can use the **distance scale** to find out. This distance scale tells you that 1 inch on this map means 1 mile in the real neighborhood.

Use a ruler to measure the distance from Sandra's house to Lisa's house. Their houses are 1 inch apart. That means Sandra lives 1 mile from Lisa.

Now measure the distance from Oscar's house to Lisa's house.

1. How many inches apart are their houses on the map?
2. How many miles is Oscar's house from Lisa's house in the neighborhood?

Review

Use New Words

1. Tell what the word **neighborhood** means.

2. Name two ways a neighborhood can **change.**

3. Which is bigger, a neighborhood or a **community**?

4. What can you see in a **suburb**?

5. How are your **neighbors** like neighbors all over the world?

Use New Ideas

6. If you were Ben Franklin, how would you help your neighborhood?

7. Why is recycling important?

8. What do you think your neighborhood will be like in the year 2040?

Think About What You Know

Where can you do these things in your neighborhood?

buy an orange   study spelling
get help   mail a letter
play softball   borrow a book

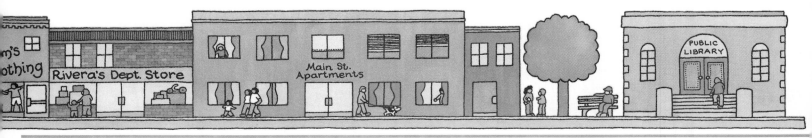

Use New Skills

Answer the questions. Use the compass rose, the map key, and the distance scale.

9. Is David's house east or west of the school?
10. Is Julia's house north or south of High Street?
11. How many inches apart are David's house and Julia's house on the map?
12. How many miles is David's house from Julia's house in the neighborhood?

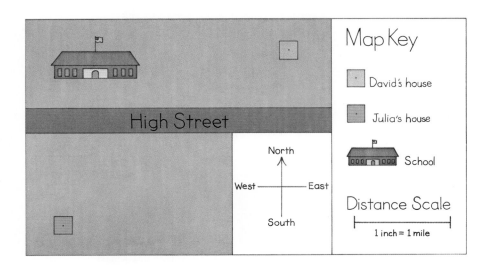

High Street

North
West —|— East
South

Map Key

David's house

Julia's house

School

Distance Scale
|—————————|
1 inch = 1 mile

Something to Do

Make a book showing the places in your neighborhood. Share your book with someone who visits you.

My Neighborhood
Library
My School

Where do names come from?

Your last name could mean something. It could be part of the **history** of your family.

History is the story of the way things happened in the past. What do you think your last name means?

Town names have a history, too. Some towns were named for the first person who lived there. Some towns were named for the way they once looked. Many towns have American Indian names. American Indians often named places for what they saw.

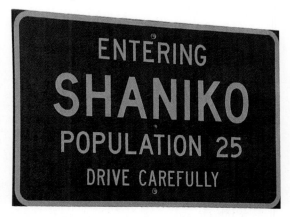

Share this story. Find out more about American Indians and the names they gave to the months of the year.

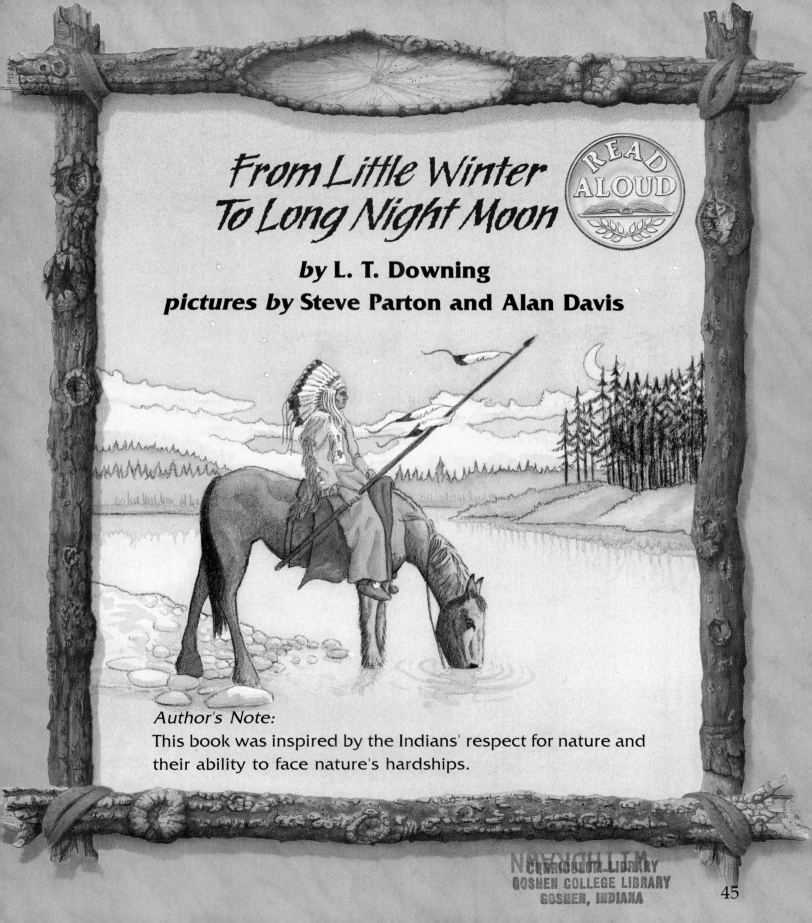

From Little Winter To Long Night Moon

READ ALOUD

by **L. T. Downing**
pictures by **Steve Parton and Alan Davis**

Author's Note:
This book was inspired by the Indians' respect for nature and their ability to face nature's hardships.

January

Little Winter
Seminole

Great bird in flight
Soars across the sun.
His silent feathers spread
Shadows on the water.

February

Snow-It-Is-White
Pawnee

A white blanket covers the plains.
Buffalo wander in search of grass
Beneath the white blanket.
Their tired footprints make circles in the snow.

Little Frog Moon
Omaha

Pull tight! Hold on!

Wild horse jumps high! Kicks low!

Pull tight! Hold on!

Wild horse! The strongest animal we know.

Fish Become Visible
Winnebago

I hear the fish's song
Of watery bubbles.
Pup-pup, pup-pup, pup-pup-pup.

Rivers Start Running

Eskimo

How many days to float down this river
Where the water is full of fish?
There my family will find food.
There my family will celebrate.

June

Cactus Fruits Are Gathered
Yumi

Grandmother picks the fruit of the cactus.

It tastes like the sun.

So warm.

When Berries Are Ripe

Plains Indian

Our work is not done, Little One.
On the grassy hills ahead,
There in the sun,
The buffalos wait for you.
Move on, Little One.
Tomorrow is yours.

August

Highest Sun

Eastern Woodlands Indian

With their cries and beating wings,
The birds scare the corn.
Our noise stirs them—Fly away! Fly away!
But our work never ends.

September

Leaves Turn Yellow
Crow

Sizzle, sizzle in a pan,
Piki bread.
Corn food for my family,
Piki bread.

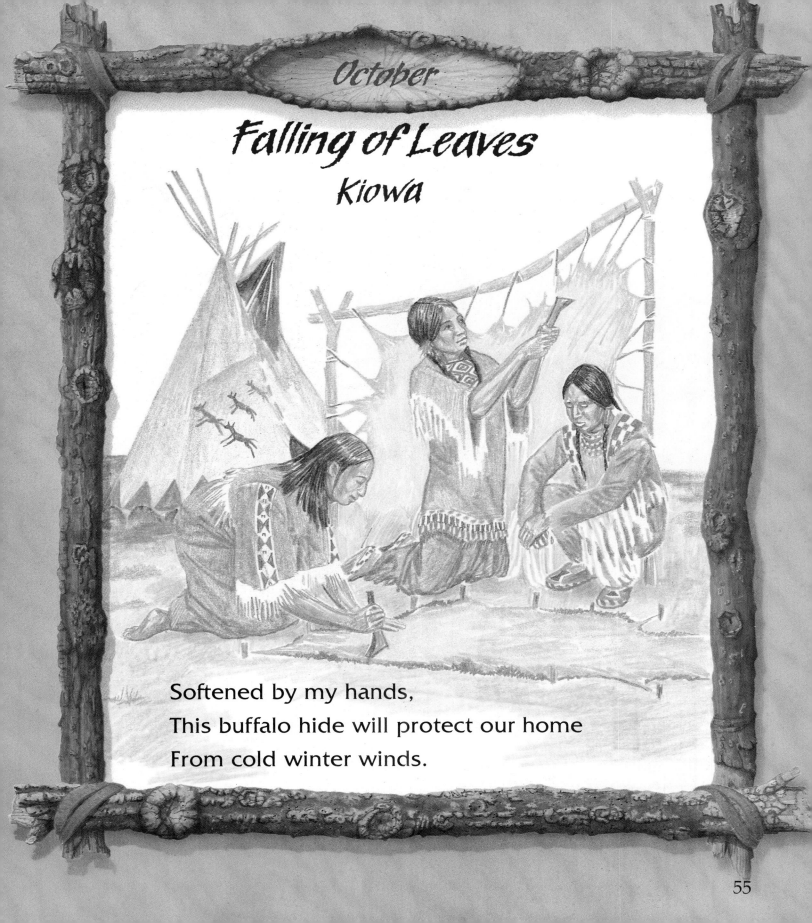

October

Falling of Leaves
Kiowa

Softened by my hands,
This buffalo hide will protect our home
From cold winter winds.

When First Snow Falls
Crow

This morning there was frost on the grass.

Mother sent us out for more wood.

Tonight our home will be warm.

Tonight the cold will stay away from our sleep.

Long Night Moon

Plains Indian

The Earth is home to all people.

It gives us fire and food.

It gives us laughing days of play.

It gives us long, quiet nights of rest.

It holds us together.

The Earth sings out in happiness.

We sing out in happiness, too.

What can I learn from this story?

The first people who lived in America were American Indians. They lived in many places all over the land.

There were many groups of American Indians. Each group was special. Each had its own ways of speaking and gathering food and building houses.

How did Indians use the land?

Our country is very large. It has many different kinds of land. Indians used the land wherever they lived. They used the animals and the trees they found on the land.

Some Indians lived in towns. They made their homes from tree bark.

Some Indians moved from place to place. They made their homes from animal skins.

Indians got their food in different ways. Some planted **crops.** Some caught fish. Some hunted wild animals. Some gathered wild fruit from trees and bushes. Other Indians got food in all these ways.

Think About This

Why do you think Indians lived in different ways?

How did Indians go from place to place?

Indians walked, swam, and rode horses to go from place to place. Sometimes Indians used canoes to travel on the water.

Here is a song they sang when they paddled their canoes.

Canoe Song

My pad - dle's keen and bright, Flash-ing with sil - ver.

Fol - low the wild goose flight, Dip, dip, and swing.

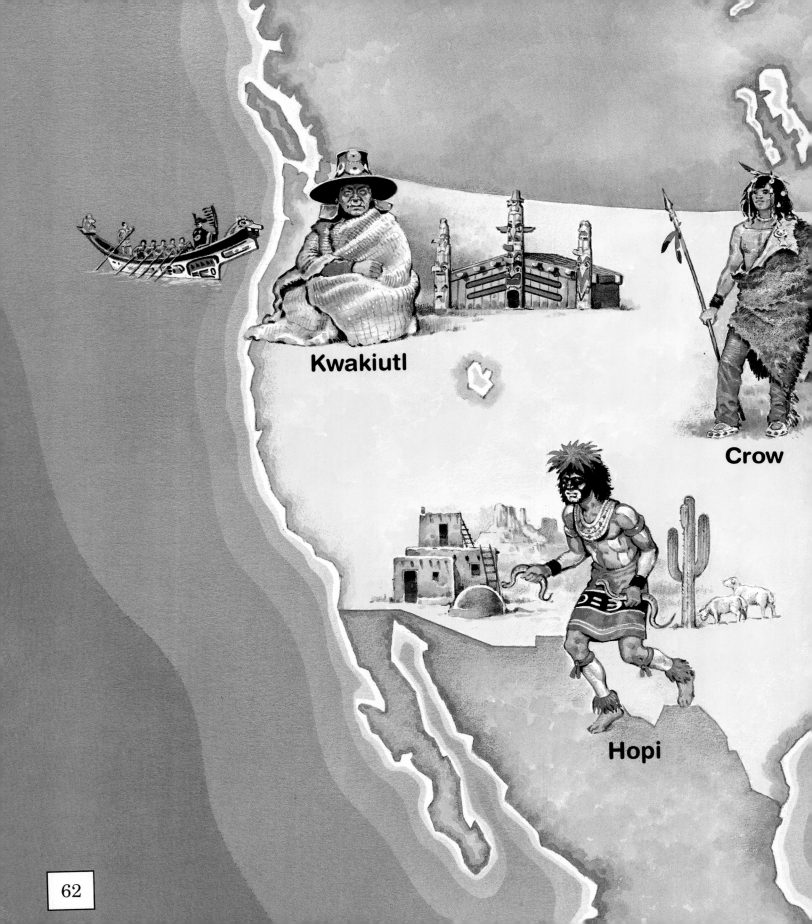

Kwakiutl

Crow

Hopi

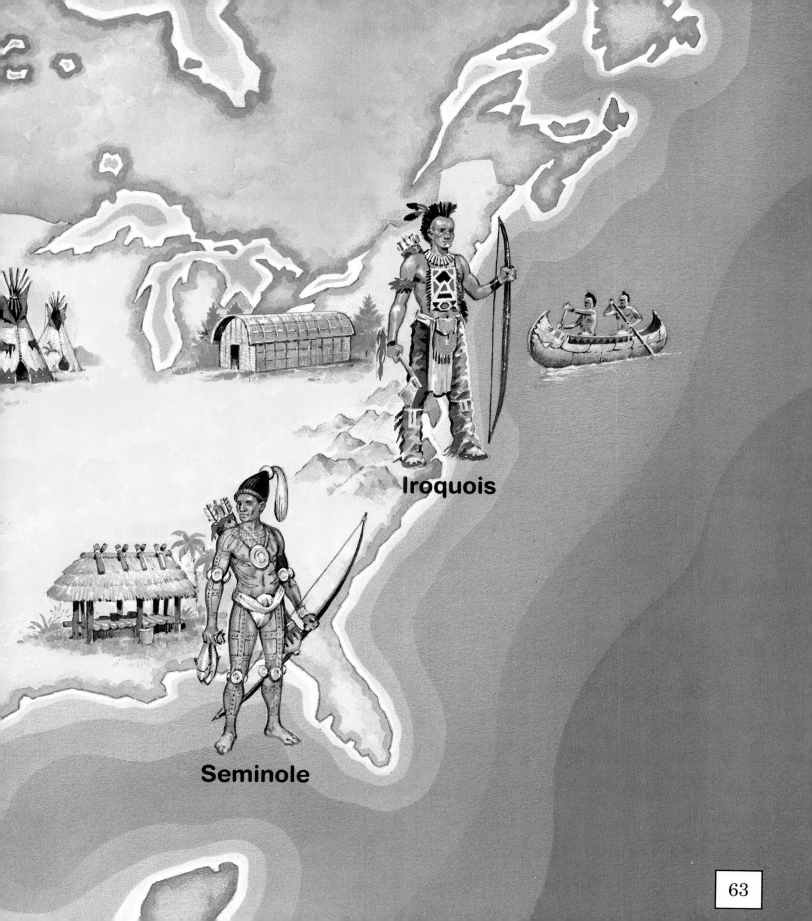

Iroquois

Seminole

63

How did other Americans get here?

Long ago, in a place called Europe, people did not know about America. In 1492 Christopher Columbus left Europe and sailed across the Atlantic Ocean. He reached the land we call America. When Columbus went back to Europe, he told people about the land he had found.

People in the countries of Europe began to learn about America. They heard that there was enough land for everyone. Some people moved to America. They left their homes and sailed across the ocean. These people were called **settlers.** Early settlers came to America from Spain, France, Holland, and Sweden.

People from England also sailed to America. These settlers built a new community in Virginia. It was called Jamestown. They planted grain and vegetables. They had to work hard to make their community grow. The Powhatan Indians helped them.

The Pilgrims were another group from England. They settled in Plymouth, Massachusetts. They lived near the Wampanoag Indians. The Indians showed the Pilgrims how to grow crops.

The Pilgrims thanked the Indians. They shared a big dinner. This was the first Thanksgiving.

Think About This

What if you were a Pilgrim? What kind of help would you want from your Indian neighbors?

More and more settlers came to America. Soon they lived in **colonies** all along the Atlantic Ocean. There were new farming villages and fishing towns. Cities began to grow near the ocean ports.

There were 13 colonies that belonged to England. This meant that the people in the 13 colonies had to follow the laws of England.

Some of these laws were unfair. The colonists did not like England's laws. They wanted to make their own laws.

The people in the 13 colonies fought England and won their **freedom.** Freedom meant that they no longer had to take orders from England. Now they were free to make their own laws.

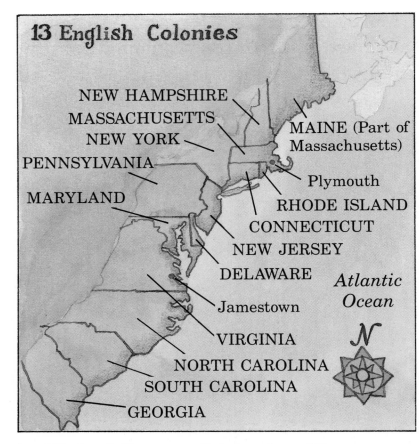

The 13 colonies became 13 states. They formed a new country. They called it the United States of America. They made a **flag** with 13 stripes and 13 stars for the 13 states.

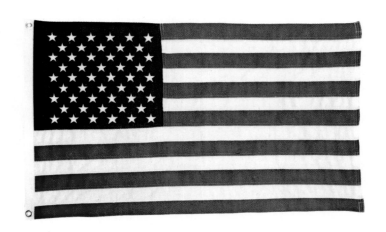

Today our flag still has 13 stripes, but it has 50 stars for 50 states.

The people asked George Washington to be their leader. They asked him to be the first **President** of the United States.

Americans celebrate winning their freedom every year on the Fourth of July. This holiday is called Independence Day.

Where did new settlers go?

Some Americans wanted to move west. There was a lot of land to be settled in the west. People needed maps and trails to find their way west.

Thomas Jefferson was the third President of the United States. He asked two **explorers** for help. Explorers are people who go ahead of others into new lands. President Jefferson asked the explorers to make a trail across the country to the far west. He asked them to make maps. The explorers were Meriwether Lewis and William Clark.

An American Indian helped them. She was Sacajawea, a Shoshone woman.

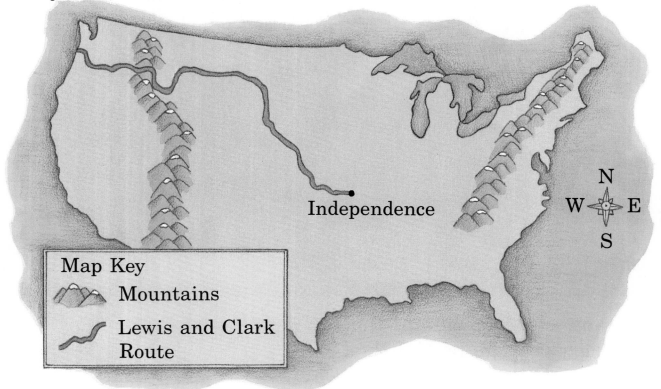

Independence

N
W E
S

Map Key

Mountains

Lewis and Clark Route

PEOPLE
to Know
About

Sacajawea's Great Adventure

One spring nearly 40 men began a journey across the country. Their goal was to explore the lands west to the Pacific Ocean. They had to cross the great western mountains. Sacajawea helped guide them.

"Don't worry," Sacajawea told them. "I know this land. Soon we will come to where the river goes three ways."

On and on they went. When the weather became cold, Sacajawea helped the men make warm clothes. When they could not find food, Sacajawea found it for them.

Finally after one and one-half years, they came to the Pacific Ocean. Their long journey was over. Sacajawea had led the way west.

Skills in Action

Sometimes we show the order in which things happen on a **timeline.** Look at this timeline. It shows the 12 months of the year. January is the first month of the year. December is the last month.

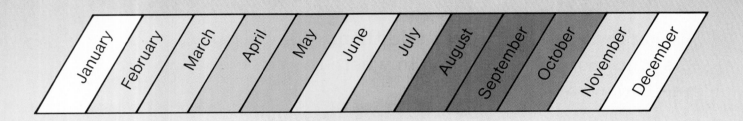

Look at the timeline and answer the questions.

1. Which month comes after April and before June?

2. Which month comes after October and before December?

3. Which month comes later in the year, September or October?

This timeline shows the birthdays of five great Americans who lived long ago. The red marks show where their birthdays fall on the calendar. The timeline helps you see the order of the birthdays during the year.

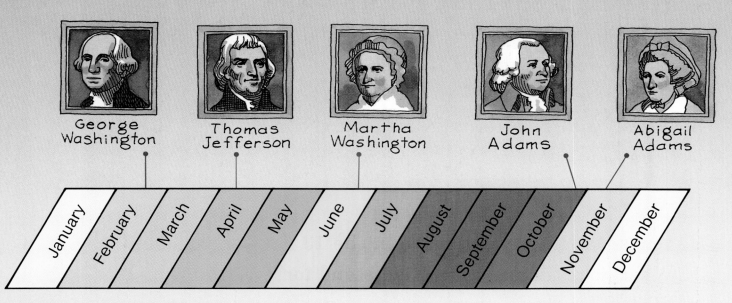

Look at the timeline and answer the questions.

1. Whose birthday is in October?
2. Whose birthday is in June?
3. Whose birthday is in February?
4. How many birthdays are there in April?
5. Who has the last birthday of the year?

Review

Use New Words

1. Tell what the word **history** means.
2. What did **crops** have to do with the first Thanksgiving?
3. Where were the 13 **colonies**?
4. How did **explorers** help the **settlers**?
5. Name two **Presidents** of the United States.

Use New Ideas

6. What was life like long ago in the 13 English colonies?
7. What does the American flag stand for?
8. Why is freedom important?
9. If new settlers came to your community, how would you help them?

Think About What You Know

Talk about American Indians and these ideas.

loved nature

helped settlers

had their own ways of speaking

named places for what they saw

traveled by canoe

lived in many parts of America

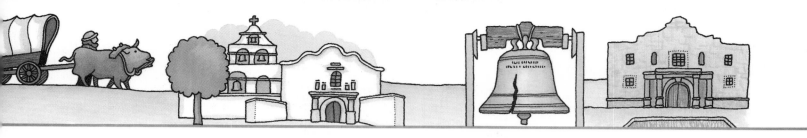

Use New Skills

This is Patricia's timeline. It shows what happened to her last year.

Look at the timeline and answer the questions.

10. What did Patricia do in June and September?
11. What did Patricia do in February and December?

Something to Do

Make your own timeline. Put your special days on it.

75

Places People Work

What kind of work did people do long ago?

The work people did long ago was not the same as the work most people do today. Long ago in the United States, most people lived and worked on family farms.

Share this story. Find out how one family lived and worked long ago.

OX-CART MAN

By DONALD HALL
Pictures by BARBARA COONEY

In October he backed his ox into his cart
and he and his family filled it up
with everything they made or grew all year long
that was left over.

He packed a bag of wool
he sheared from the sheep in April.

He packed a shawl his wife wove on a loom
from yarn spun at the spinning wheel
from sheep sheared in April.

He packed five pairs of mittens
his daughter knit
from yarn spun at the spinning wheel
from sheep sheared in April.

He packed candles the family made.

He packed linen made from flax they grew.

He packed shingles he split himself.

He packed birch brooms his son carved
with a borrowed kitchen knife.

He packed potatoes they dug from their garden
— but first he counted out potatoes enough to eat all winter
and potatoes for seed next spring.

He packed a barrel of apples
honey and honeycombs
turnips and cabbages
a wooden box of maple sugar
from the maples they tapped in March
when they boiled and boiled and boiled the sap away.
He packed a bag of goose feathers that his children collected
from the barnyard geese.

When his cart was full, he waved good-bye to his wife,
his daughter, and his son
and he walked at his ox's head ten days
over hills, through valleys, by streams
past farms and villages
until he came to Portsmouth
and Portsmouth Market.

He sold the bag of wool.

He sold the shawl his wife made.

He sold five pairs of mittens.

He sold candles and shingles.

He sold birch brooms.

He sold potatoes.

He sold apples.

He sold honey and honeycombs,
turnips and cabbages.

He sold maple sugar.

He sold a bag of goose feathers.

Then he sold the wooden box he carried the maple sugar in.

Then he sold the barrel he carried the apples in.

Then he sold the bag he carried the potatoes in.

Then he sold his ox cart.

Then he sold his ox, and kissed him good-bye on his nose.

Then he sold his ox's yoke and harness.

With his pockets full of coins, he walked through Portsmouth Market.

He bought an iron kettle to hang over the fire at home,

and for his daughter he bought an embroidery needle
that came from a boat in the harbor
that had sailed all the way from England,

and for his son he bought a Barlow knife,
for carving birch brooms with

and for the whole family he bought two pounds
of wintergreen peppermint candies.

Then he walked home, with the needle and the knife
and the wintergreen peppermint candies tucked into the
kettle,

and a stick over his shoulder, stuck through the kettle's handle,
and coins still in his pockets,

past farms and villages,
over hills, through valleys, by streams,

until he came to his farm,
and his son, his daughter, and his wife were waiting for him,

and his daughter took her needle and began stitching,

and his son took his Barlow knife and started whittling,

and they cooked dinner in their new kettle,

and afterward everyone ate a wintergreen peppermint candy,

and that night the ox-cart man sat in front of his fire
stitching new harness
for the young ox in the barn

and he carved a new yoke

and sawed planks for a new cart

and split shingles all winter,

while his wife made flax into linen all winter,

and his daughter embroidered linen all winter,

and his son carved Indian brooms from birch all winter,

and everybody made candles,

and in March they tapped the sugar maple trees
and boiled the sap down,

and in April they sheared the sheep,

spun yarn,

and wove and knitted,

and in May they planted potatoes, turnips, and cabbages,

while apple blossoms bloomed and fell,

while bees woke up, starting to make new honey,

and geese squawked in the barnyard,

dropping feathers as soft as clouds.

What can I learn from this story?

The Ox-Cart Man and his family met most of their needs on their farm. They grew their own food and made their own clothes. They made some things to sell. They sold the extra food they grew.

Long ago, people met their needs the way the Ox-Cart Man did. Today people meet their needs in different ways.

All people have **needs.** Needs are things that people cannot live without.

Think About This

What needs do all people have?

What are the most important needs?

Everyone needs food, water, clothing, and shelter. They were the most important needs for the Ox-Cart Man. They are the most important needs today.

The place we live in is our shelter. Our shelter is our home. People live in all kinds of homes.

Every home begins with a plan. An architect draws a plan to show what a house will look like. The plan shows the different parts of a house. It shows how the parts will fit together.

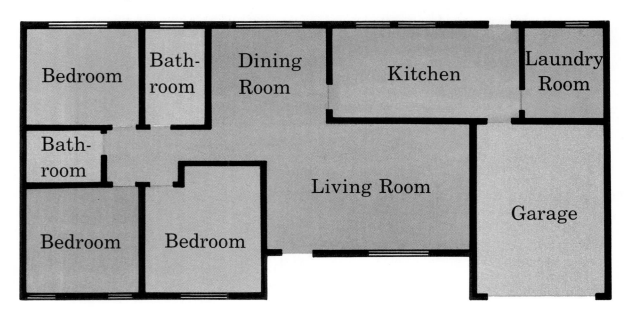

Many workers use the plan. Their job is to put together the different parts of the house.

These are some parts of a house.

| walls | windows | wires for lights | chimney |
| floors | doors | pipes for water | roof |

Every worker does a different job. One job follows another so the house will be put together right.

Is this house like the Ox-Cart Man's house?

Where does our food come from today?

The Ox-Cart Man and his family grew the food they needed. Today most of our food comes from large farms. Farmers grow vegetables, fruit, and grain. They raise chickens, cows, and other animals. They sell some of the crops and meat to stores. Then we buy the food in stores.

Some farm crops must be made into food before we can buy them. Some farmers grow wheat that is made into flour. The flour goes to a bakery where it is baked into bread.

Farmers send some crops, such as peaches, to canneries. Canneries are places where foods are put into cans.

Think About This

What if all the stores ran out of fruits and vegetables? How would you get food?

How is clothing made today?

Just like the Ox-Cart Man, we get wool from sheep. We also get cotton from cotton plants. Today machines spin wool and cotton into thread. Then machines weave the thread into cloth.

The cloth is sent to factories. There, workers cut it up using patterns. They sew the pieces into clothes. Then the clothes are sent to stores.

PEOPLE
to Know
About

Mr. Ward and His Mail-Order Store

Montgomery Ward worked for a store in
St. Louis, Missouri, around the year 1870. He
went all over the countryside trying to sell goods
to farm families.

Everywhere he went, he carried large rolls of cloth,
samples of clothes, ribbons, needles, and thread.

The farmers and their families looked at the things
and thought they were nice. But the goods cost too
much, and the people could not buy them.

Montgomery wanted to help farm families buy things they wanted and needed. One day he had an idea. He would start his own business. He would lower the cost of goods so that the farm families could buy them.

Montgomery opened a small office in Chicago. He printed a one-page list of the things he had for sale. Montgomery sent the list to all the farmers he knew. He gave directions on how to order by mail.

The farmers and their families liked Montgomery Ward's mail-order business. Within a few years, the one-page list became a catalog with hundreds of pages and pictures. Montgomery Ward started a new way to shop. For more than 100 years, people used his catalog to shop.

What are wants?

The Ox-Cart Man wanted to buy things at the market. **Wants** are things that people would like to have. Wants are not as important as needs. We do not have to have them to live.

Think About This

Most things that people need or want must be bought. What do we use to pay for things?

How do people get money?

Families earn money by working. Money that families get from working is called **income.** The Ox-Cart Man sold the things he and his family made. This earned them money to buy the things they wanted and needed. This money was income for the Ox-Cart Man's family.

How are these people earning an income?

Some people earn an income by selling **goods.** Goods are things that people make or grow. Some workers grow the food we eat. Some workers make the things we use.

The Ox-Cart Man and his family did most things for themselves. Some people today pay to have things done for them. **Services** are jobs that workers do for others.

What services do these people provide?

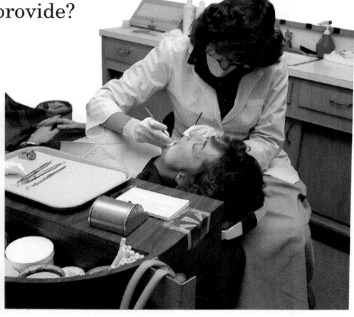

Think About This

What services do workers provide in your community?

What work do people do in other countries?

People in other countries have jobs. Their jobs may be just like jobs in this country.

People in other countries work in factories where goods are made. Many people in other countries work to grow food. They grow some of the same foods that we enjoy.

People need the same things no matter what country they live in. Their ways of getting them are often the same, too.

Nearly all people use money to pay for things they want and need. But another way to get things is to **barter.** Barter means to trade one thing for another.

How do people decide what to do with their money?

People use some of their money to pay for their needs and some to pay for their wants. People **save** some money, too. People save so they will have money for things they will need and want in the future.

How are these people using their savings?

Many people save their money by taking it to a special place. Banks, credit unions, and savings and loans are special places for saving money.

Do people always earn an income from work?

Some people do not earn an income from some of their work. These people are **volunteers.**

Volunteers give their services for free. They do this because they want to help other people. They want to be good neighbors and good members of their communities.

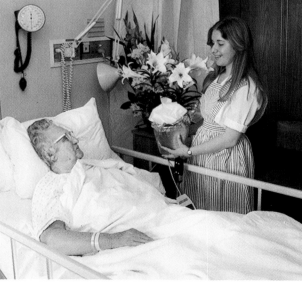

How are these people helping?

PLACES
to Know
About

A Special Playground

Volunteers have built a playground where all children can play together. This playground is called the "All Children's Playground," and it is in Orlando, Florida.

The playground is for children who can walk and for children who cannot. It is for children who can stand and for children who cannot. It is for children who cannot see or hear and for those who can.

Jeanne and Steve were the leaders of the team of volunteers. Cheryl asked schoolchildren what should go in the playground. Donna took charge of the design. Jim planned the building of the playground.

John and Helen told everyone when to come to help. Tom and Gloria bought the wood and the nails. Cindy brought the food. Mariann and Linda took care of small children so that their parents could help.

More people came than could be counted. They hammered and sawed and built the playground. Everyone worked together so all children could play together.

Skills in Action

Look at the picture. Count the trees, houses, and cars.

Below is a special kind of picture. It shows the number of things. It is called a **bar graph.** Find the pictures across the bottom. The pictures tell you what is being counted. Now look at the numbers on the left side. The numbers tell you how many there are. The colored bar goes up to the right number.

Put your finger on the picture of the car. Move your finger up to the top of the bar. The bar stops at 3. This tells you that there are three cars in the picture. Do the same for the house and the tree.

114

Look at the bar graph below. It shows what the Ox-Cart Man took to market. Find the bar that shows how many brooms there were. The bar stops at the number 2. The Ox-Cart Man took two brooms to market.

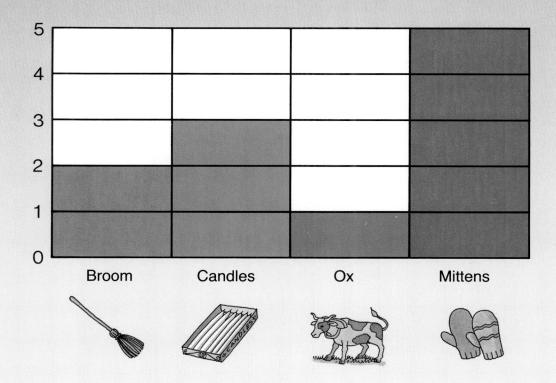

Look at the bar graph again and answer the questions.

1. How many boxes of candles are there?
2. How many pairs of mittens are there?
3. Is there more than one ox?
4. Are there more brooms or more pairs of mittens?
5. Are there more boxes of candles or more brooms?

If you made a bar graph, what would you show?

Review

Use New Words

1. How are **needs** and **wants** different?
2. How did the Ox-Cart Man get his **income**?
3. How are **goods** and **services** alike?
4. Tell what it means to **barter.**
5. Why do **volunteers** work for free?

Use New Ideas

6. Name two ways you could earn money.
7. What is a good reason to save money?
8. Where can people save money?
9. Why is it important to earn an income?
10. How do you think people in the future will earn an income?

Think About What You Know

Which are needs and which are wants?

| shelter | water | shoes | marbles |
| vegetables | ring | teddy bear | milk |

Use New Skills

Look at the bar graph and answer the questions.

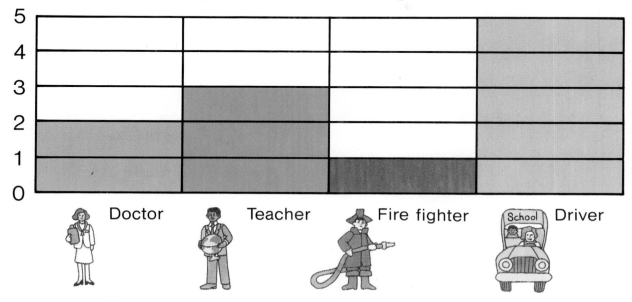

11. How many teachers are there?
12. How many fire fighters are there?
13. Are there more doctors or more drivers?

Something to Do

Make a list of the jobs you do for other people in one week. Then make a bar graph to show these services and how many times you provided them.

Tuesday
• Help clean playground

Wednesday
• Plant flowers

Thursday helpers:
Jeff
Roland
Megan

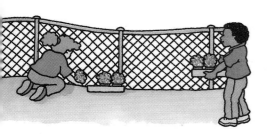

Places and Choices

How do I get along in groups?

During your life you will belong to many different **groups.** Groups are people doing things together. Your family is a group that you will be part of all your life. Your class is a group that lasts for the school year. When you go to see a baseball game, you are part of a group for a few hours.

You and your neighbors are a group. People in groups must work together. They must work to get along with each other.

Read this story about how some people learned to get along together.

What Can You Do With a Statue?

by Jerdine Nolen Harold

illustrated by Sally Schaedler

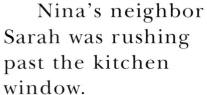

Nina's neighbor Sarah was rushing past the kitchen window.

"Sarah," Nina called, "aren't you going to stop for a while?"

"Not today, Nina. I must get to the park. We have a big problem. Someone wants to take the statue of Sam Smith out of the park!"

"Who would want to do a thing like that?" Nina said with surprise. "That statue has been there forever! This town wouldn't be the same without it!"

"That's just what I think," Sarah said. "That's why I'm going over to the park, and quick!"

"Wait!" called Nina. "I'm coming with you!"

Nina and Sarah rushed to the park. Even before they got there they could see a crowd forming. People were gathered around the statue of Sam Smith.

"It's time for this statue to come down," said a man. "We need something new and up-to-date!"

"I agree," said Jake the barber. "I have lived here all my life and so has that statue. I am tired of seeing it."

"Me too," shouted Kim, a student from the town's high school. "A new statue would look much better."

"I say no," said Bill, the park's grounds keeper. "Why, that statue's like an old friend."

"What is wrong with having a new friend?" someone said. "You might like a new statue just as well as the old one!"

One lady spoke up. "I like this statue. I sit on the park bench right next to it and eat my lunch on sunny days."

Nina didn't like what she was seeing and hearing.

"These people, who are good friends, are not getting along!" she thought to herself.

"Everyone in the whole town is mad at one another. Each person seems sure he or she is right. The problem is that no one has a chance to hear what anyone else is saying."

Looking up at Sam Smith's statue, Nina thought he looked very sad.

Nina heard herself shout, "The people should decide!"
To Nina's surprise the voices were quieting down as
people looked her way.

"We need to find a fair way to solve this problem," Nina
went on.

"I have an idea. Let's put this to a vote! The side that gets the most votes will choose whether or not the statue stays," said Nina.

Well, that seemed like a good idea to everyone.

Looking up at the statue, Nina thought that Sam Smith looked like he might be smiling.

"Just maybe he *is* smiling," thought Nina as she chuckled to herself.

"All in favor of keeping the statue in the park, raise your hands and be counted."

Jake and two others counted and then counted again before recording the vote.

"All in favor of getting a new statue, raise your hands and be counted."

Carefully, the votes were counted and counted again.

133

"It's a tie vote!" said Kim in surprise. "Neither side got any more votes than the other."

"This is worse!" said Jake.

"We're no better off now than we were before!" said Sarah.

"I think you are wrong," Nina said with a smile.

"Don't you see? The vote shows that people want two things. Some want an old statue, and some people want a new statue that keeps up with the times! Why not have both?"

"Now, where can we put the new statue?" Jake chimed in happily.

"Let's put it to a vote!" laughed Nina.

And they did!

What can I learn from this story?

People in groups sometimes **vote** to decide what to do. Voting is fair. Voting lets each person have a say. How did voting help the people in the story?

People solve problems by working together.
Nina and her friends talked and voted.
They worked together to solve their problem.

Statues are a part of America. We have statues to help us remember people. Some statues remind us of things that happened long ago.

The Statue of Liberty

The Statue of Liberty is a famous American statue. It is a symbol of the United States. In the 1980s, Americans wanted to celebrate the statue's 100th birthday. But they worried about the statue. It was worn and cracked and stained. It needed repairs inside and outside.

People wondered what to do. Fixing the statue would cost a lot of money. But if they left it alone, the statue would get worse. It might even break and fall apart. Americans decided to fix the statue. Men and women and girls and boys all over the country gave money to fix the statue.

The leaders asked engineers and artists how to fix the statue. The experts said that they would have to take the statue apart. Workers took some pieces to special workshops. They fixed the crown and the torch. They cleaned the head. They made the body of the statue strong inside and outside.

At last everything was ready. The pieces were put back together. All the work was done in time for the statue's 100th birthday. Americans held a big party for the Statue of Liberty on the Fourth of July, 1986.

Why do I have to follow rules?

All groups have **rules.** Rules tell us what to do and what not to do. There are reasons for rules. Some rules keep us safe. Some rules help us get along with one another. Some rules keep things fair for all people.

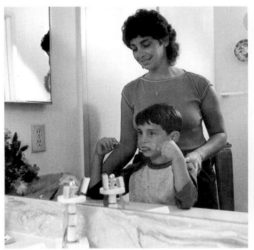

Each family has its own rules. Schools have rules, too. What rules are these children following?

What are laws?

Laws are rules for everyone. All people in each community need to obey the laws. All communities have laws about safety. There are laws about traffic and laws about pets. Laws help people get along together.

Think About This

What might happen if people did not obey these laws?

141

Laws help people solve problems. They help make a community a better place for everyone. Some laws are against littering. Some laws are about recycling garbage.

Think About This

How do laws about garbage help a community?

Who makes the laws?

People in **government** make laws. It is one of their jobs.

City laws are made by leaders who work in city government. The city lawmakers work at **City Hall.** They work together at city council meetings. In many cities, the **mayor** is the most important city leader.

Congress is part of the country's government. Congress makes laws for the United States. Americans vote for people to be members of Congress. Congress meets in the **Capitol Building** in Washington, D.C.

Washington, D.C., is the **capital** of our country. The capital is the city where government is. The Capitol Building and the White House are in the capital city. The White House is where the President lives. The President is the leader of the United States.

Who makes sure our country's laws are fair?

The Supreme Court is the most important court in the United States. Nine judges are on the Supreme Court. They decide whether the nation's laws are fair. The Supreme Court is in Washington, D.C.

PEOPLE to Know About

Sandra Day O'Connor—Judge on the Supreme Court

Sandra Day O'Connor finished high school in Texas and college in California. She was one of the best students in her class. Later she became a lawyer.

People voted for her, and she became a senator in Arizona. In 1981 President Ronald Reagan named her to the Supreme Court.

Sandra Day O'Connor is the first woman to be a judge on the Supreme Court.

You see many signs like these in your neighborhood.

1. Which sign tells a driver to stop the car?
2. Which sign tells you to use a different door?
3. Which sign tells you to be quiet?
4. Which sign tells you not to go into that yard?
5. Which sign tells you not to cross the street?
6. Which sign tells you that your dog must wait outside?

a.

b.

c.

d.

e.

f.

Some signs do not use words. They use symbols. Have you ever seen this symbol? It tells you where you can make a telephone call.

Sometimes you see a symbol with a line through it. This means that you cannot do something. You cannot take your dog into a place where you see this sign.

Which of these signs have you seen? What do they mean?

Are there laws in other countries?

Countries all over the world have their own laws.

Signs help people in other countries. They tell people what to do and what not to do to be safe.

In some countries there are meetings
where laws are made for the whole country.

Think About This

Suppose you travel to other countries. Whose
laws would you follow, ours or theirs?

Review

Use New Words

1. Tell how a **group** can decide things.
2. What is one job of **government**?
3. What is the difference between a **rule** and a **law**?
4. How is **City Hall** like the **Capitol Building**?
5. What will you find in the **capital** of the United States?

Use New Ideas

6. Do families make rules or laws?
7. How has your vote changed something?
8. If you become President, what will you do for your country?

Think About What You Know

Tell which of these words are about city government
and which are about the United States government.

mayor   City Hall   Capitol Building
capital   Supreme Court   Congress

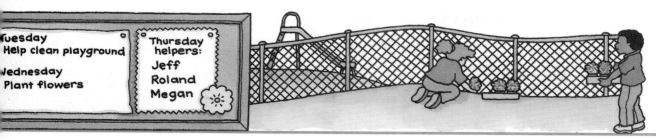

Use New Skills

The people in these pictures are all obeying laws and rules. Find the sign that belongs in each picture.

9.

10.

11.

12.

13.

a. STOP

b. DON'T BE A LITTERBUG

c. WAIT YOUR TURN

d. DO NOT WALK

e.

Something to Do

Draw a sign for a new law. Only use symbols. Show your sign to a friend. Ask your friend to guess what your sign means.

Where do Americans live?

Almost every American lives in a **state.** A state is one part of the United States. A state is made up of many cities and towns. Your neighborhood is in a state.

Every state has its own name and its own history.

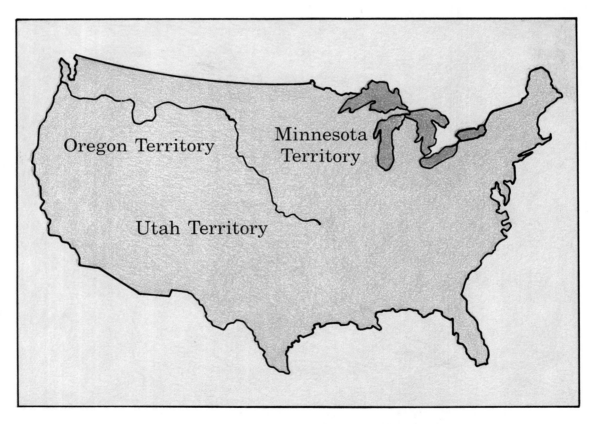

Read the play The Cleanest Town in the West. The play is about a make-believe gang who went to Oregon long ago. The play takes place a few years before Oregon became a state.

The Cleanest Town in the West

NARRATORS

Historian
Reporter
Spectator

ACTORS

The Onion Gang	Merchant
John Onion	Carmelita
Apple Alice	Dirty Dan
Ringo	Miner #1
Grocery Clerk	Miner #2
Sheriff	Miner #3

Townsfolk

words by Caron Lee Cohen
sets by Michael Latoria
styled by Trudy Bruner

SCENE 1
PLACE AND TIME: MAIN STREET IN SUNRISE VALLEY, OREGON,
AUGUST 10, 1858.

HISTORIAN: Sunrise Valley was a beautiful town. Everything was very clean until the Onion Gang rode into town.

JOHN ONION: (showing off) I'm wild and wooly and full of fleas! And this is my day to howl, Whoopee!

[John Onion tosses his hat in the air. Ringo throws some paper on the ground.]

GROCERY CLERK: Don't do that to our streets!

RINGO: Well, I'll be a cow in a pigpen! It's only a little paper.

SHERIFF: This is a good, clean town. We don't want rowdy folks. We have laws, you know.

TOWNSFOLK: **This town is good, this town is best; this town's the cleanest in the West!**

APPLE ALICE: I'm so hungry, I could eat a horse.

JOHN ONION: (to Ringo) Get Alice an apple.

[Ringo takes an apple from the pile in front of the grocery store.]

GROCERY CLERK: Thieves! Thieves!

SHERIFF: I'll get you once and for all! (grabbing Ringo) Now give back the apple, or pay for it!

[Ringo hands the apple to the Sheriff.]

TOWNSFOLK: **This town is good, this town is best; this town's the cleanest in the West!**

SPECTATOR: The Onion Gang rode out of town in a cloud of dust. Later they stopped to rest.

RINGO: (opening a newspaper) Look at this!

APPLE ALICE: (grabbing the newspaper and reading out loud) "The Sunrise Valley News. Gold discovered in Oregon Territory!"

RINGO: Gold!

JOHN ONION: Whoopee! What else does it say?

APPLE ALICE: "Two months ago, men digging in Grizzly Gorge found gold. Miners are rushing there. A new town is going up for all the newcomers. They've named the town Red Dog. There's no mayor or sheriff in Red Dog. There's no law either."

JOHN ONION: Wow! A new mining town! No laws, no sheriff! No one to run us out! It's our kind of town. Let's get going!

SCENE 2
PLACE AND TIME: RED DOG IN OREGON TERRITORY, FOUR DAYS LATER.

MERCHANT: (with wagon load of picks and shovels) Picks and tools for sale! Picks and tools!

[The Onion Gang rides into Red Dog looking tired and dirty.]

JOHN ONION: Whoopee! We made it! This is Red Dog! Look, the buildings are tents. I guess it takes time to build with logs.

RINGO: (laughing) It's okay to have logs, as long as they don't have laws.

[A woman throws trash in the street.]

APPLE ALICE: (happily) Sure is dirty!

TOWNSFOLK: **This town is rough, this town is tough; this town is dirty sure enough!**

[A man steals a pick off the tool wagon and runs away.]

CARMELITA: (to the merchant) I saw that. And it's wrong! He shouldn't get away with it.

MERCHANT: But what can we do?

CARMELITA: We ought to make some laws, elect a mayor, choose a sheriff!

JOHN ONION: (laughing, walking away) Whoopee! No laws, no sheriff!

APPLE ALICE: No one to tell us we're rowdy.

TOWNSFOLK: **This town is rough, this town is tough; this town is dirty sure enough!**

SPECTATOR: Ringo tripped over some chickens in the street. Horses reared up.

[**SOUND EFFECTS:** crash of things falling to the ground, chicken and horse sounds]

SPECTATOR: Someone's wagon toppled over. Everything spilled on the street. John Onion tripped and fell.

CARMELITA: (to John) Let me help you!

JOHN ONION: Oh, I hurt my knees, elbows, too.

TOWNSFOLK: (sadly) **This town is rough, this town is tough; this town is dirty sure enough!**

JOHN ONION: I wish they'd clean their street!

CARMELITA: If you're staying, it's your street too.

REPORTER: Everyone went into a restaurant. Miners were sitting and eating. John Onion took out some money.

JOHN ONION: It's my day to howl! Whoopee! I'm buying everyone a cold lemonade.

REPORTER: All of a sudden, a mean looking man, Dirty Dan, got up from a table. He walked over to John Onion. Everyone shuddered.

DIRTY DAN: I'm Dirty Dan. And I don't like anybody showing off unless it's me! Understand?

JOHN ONION: Well, I'm John Onion. And this is a free country!

DIRTY DAN: If I say you can't, you can't! The wildcats in the woods are scared of me. You better be too!
(He waves his fist.)

[Some dusty miners sit down next to the Onion Gang.]

RINGO: (to Miner #1) You look tired. Mining must be hard work.

MINER #1: In those mountains it's hard, all right. Only men and mules would do it!

MINER #2: But I struck gold! Now I'm going to build a house and send for my family.

MINER #3: This town's a little rough now, but it's giving us a chance.

APPLE ALICE: A chance—that's what we want too.

REPORTER: The Onion Gang, Carmelita, and the miners left the restaurant. They saw Dirty Dan untying the mules and running off with them.

JOHN ONION: Come on, gang. We'll get him! (reaching, grabbing Dirty Dan) Stop, thief! (to Dirty Dan) If we had a sheriff, you'd be in jail. But we don't. So just keep on running out of Red Dog. And don't ever come back!

[Dirty Dan gets on his horse and rides out.]

[**Sound Effects:** horse galloping]

Everyone: Hurrah, hurrah for John Onion!

Carmelita: We need to make some laws. Let's get everyone here for a town meeting.

John Onion: We'll clean our streets and have a great town.

Townsfolk: **This town'll be good, this town'll be best; this town'll be the cleanest in the West!**

SCENE 3
PLACE AND TIME: RED DOG, ONE YEAR LATER.

CARMELITA: Ours is the best town in the West.

APPLE ALICE: This town gave us a chance, and we all made it a great place to live.

JOHN ONION: That's right! This town is as good and clean as any!

TOWNSFOLK: **This town is good, this town's the best; this town's the cleanest in the West!**

[CURTAIN]

What can I learn from this story?

Neighbors must work together. They must take care of the places where they live. They must have laws to help them.

States have laws. A state's laws are made in a city called the capital. The capital is where the state's government works. In each state, people vote for lawmakers who work in the capital.

Think About This

What is the name of the state where you live?

Can you find your state on this map?

Find your state on the map. Which states are your closest neighbors? What is the capital of your state?

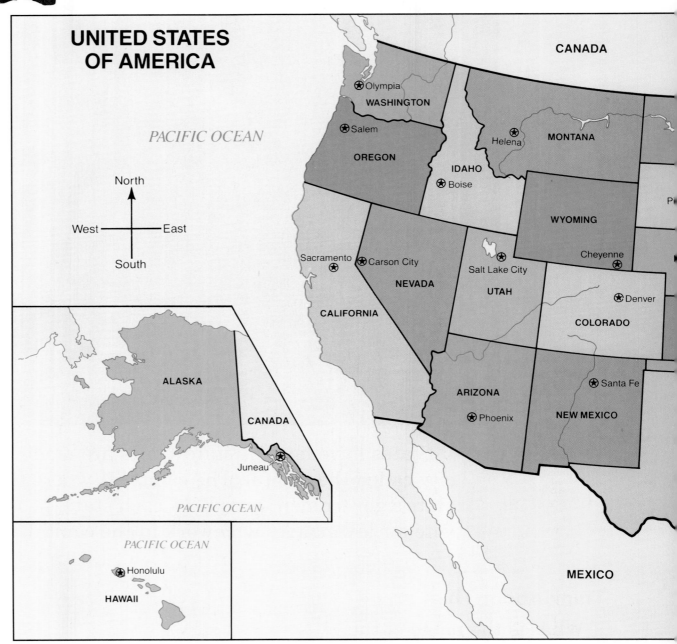

There are 50 states in the United States.
Two of these states are far from the rest of
the United States. Which states are those?

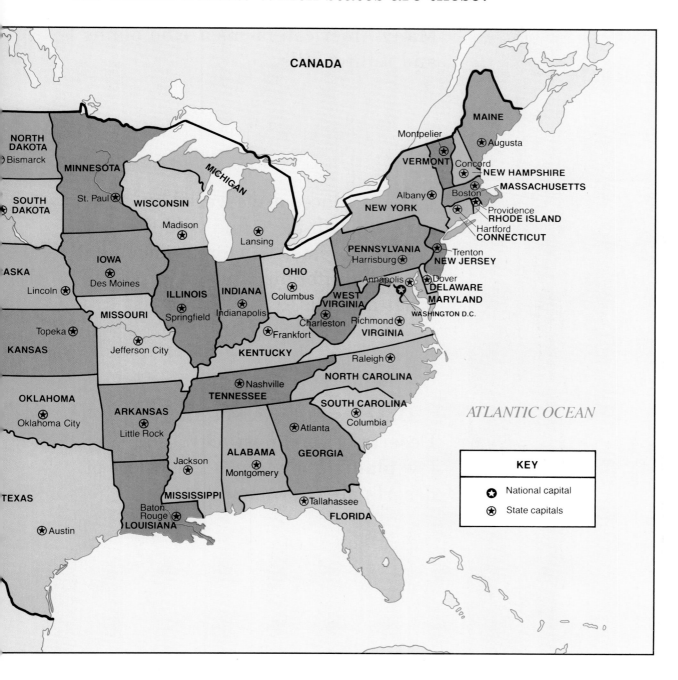

What does America look like?

Some places are flat or nearly flat. Flat lands are called **plains.** Some places have rolling hills. Many American farms are on plains and rolling hills.

Other places are covered by **forests.** Tall trees and wild flowers grow in forests. The forest is home to many different kinds of birds and other animals.

Deserts are places that are dry. Deserts have almost no water. Very few plants grow there. The colors of deserts are browns and tans.

America has many bodies of water. Lakes, rivers, and oceans are bodies of water. The fish and other seafood that people eat come from lakes, rivers, and oceans.

Oceans are larger than lakes and rivers. Oceans form the coasts of many states. The coast is where the land meets the ocean. Ocean water is salt water. Salt water is not drinking water.

Lakes and rivers have fresh water. They give us drinking water. **Lakes** have land all around them.

Rivers are long and flow through the land. All rivers are different. Some rivers are wide and some are narrow.

Think About This

Why is it important to keep our lakes, rivers, and oceans clean?

THIS LAND IS YOUR LAND

This land is your land, this land is my land

From California to the New York island,

From the redwood forest to the Gulf Stream waters;

This land was made for you and me.

As I was walking that ribbon of highway

I saw above me that endless skyway;

I saw below me that golden valley;

This land was made for you and me.

I've roamed and rambled, and I followed my footsteps

To the sparkling sands of her diamond deserts;

And all around me a voice was sounding:

This land was made for you and me.

When the sun came shining, and I was strolling,

And the wheat fields waving and the dust clouds rolling,

As the fog was lifting a voice was chanting:

This land was made for you and me.

PEOPLE to Know About

Grandma Moses and Her Wonderful Art

Anna Moses was a painter who was called "Grandma Moses." That is because she started painting when she was in her seventies. She kept painting until she was 101 years old. She painted pictures of the land she saw around her and the land she remembered from childhood. She painted the picture on page 176.

Skills in Action

Look at the map of North America on the next page.

1. Find the United States. It is in the middle of North America.

2. Find the countries that are our neighbors. Our neighbors are Canada and Mexico.

3. Find the compass rose.

4. Which country is north of the United States?

5. Which country is south of the United States?

6. Do we have neighbors to the east or the west?

7. Why is Alaska the same color as the United States?

8. What are the names of the oceans you see?

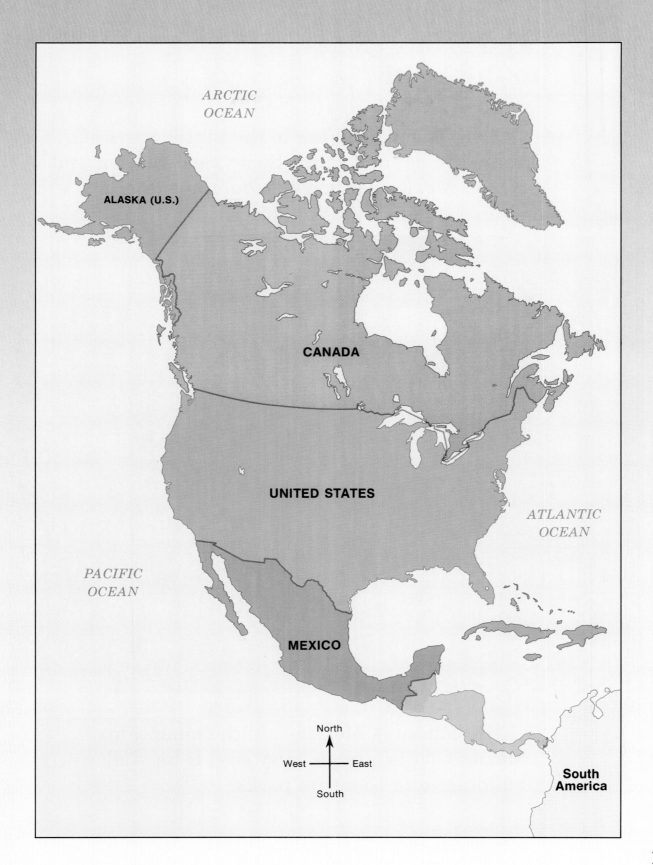

ARCTIC
OCEAN

ALASKA (U.S.)

CANADA

UNITED STATES

ATLANTIC
OCEAN

PACIFIC
OCEAN

MEXICO

North

West —— East

South

South
America

Who is our closest neighbor to the south?

Mexico is our neighbor to the south. Parts of Mexico are hot and rainy. Some parts are hot and dry. Yet Mexico has snowy mountains, too.

The capital of Mexico is in the mountains. Mexico City is a huge, busy city. It has tall buildings and beautiful parks.

In the north of Mexico there are deserts. This desert is hot during the day. It is cold at night.

This part of Mexico is always warm. People visit the beaches all year round.

This land was once a desert, too. It was very dry. The people of Mexico brought water to it. Today it is good farmland. We get many fruits and vegetables from Mexico.

Who is closest to the north?

Canada is our neighbor to the north. Many places in Canada are like places in the United States.

In this part of Canada it is cold and snowy in the winter. The snow melts in the summer. These people are Eskimos. Eskimo families have lived here for a long time.

In the middle of Canada, there are plains. Crops grow well here. Many farmers raise wheat.

In many places there are forests of tall trees. Rivers run down from the mountains and hills.

Canada has many big cities. Often these cities are near the ocean or next to rivers. The capital of Canada is Ottawa.

Canada and the United States have been good neighbors for many years.

Review

Use New Words

1. Name the capital of your **state.**
2. How are the **plains** and rolling hills alike?
3. How are **oceans** and **lakes** and **rivers** different?
4. What kinds of things live in **forests**?
5. What colors would you use to paint a picture of a **desert**?

Use New Ideas

6. Why should people save forests?
7. How are Canada and Mexico like the United States? How are they different?
8. Do you live closer to Canada or to Mexico?
9. If you could visit another country in North America, which would you choose? Tell why.

Think About What You Know

Choose the places where you could hike, swim, climb, sail, and bicycle.

| ocean | lakes | rivers | rolling hills |
| deserts | forests | plains | mountains |

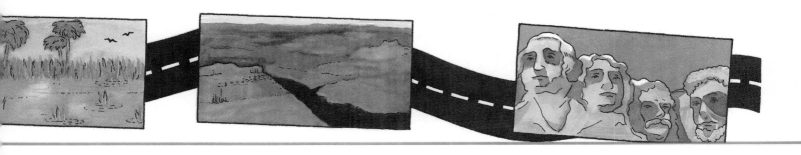

Use New Skills

Find the compass rose on the
map. Then answer the questions.

10. If you move your finger from Mexico to Canada,
    in which direction are you going?

11. If you move your finger from Canada to Mexico,
    in which direction are you going?

12. If you move your finger from the Atlantic Ocean to the
    Pacific Ocean, in which direction are you going?

13. Which country is farthest south on the map?

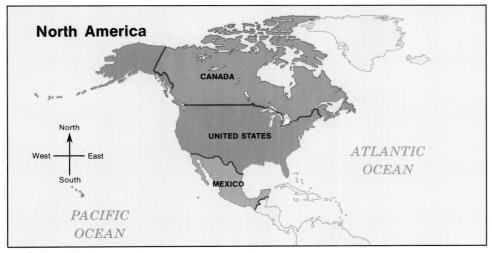

Something to Do

Find out about your state. Then make
a book about it. Share your state book
with a friend.

185

Why do Americans dress and eat in special ways?

Many Americans have come from other countries. They may not dress the way you do. They may not eat the foods you like to eat. Some Americans still wear the clothes of other countries. Some Americans still eat the foods of other countries.

Share this story about one girl's parents. It is about how her mother and father learned to eat together.

How My Parents Learned to Eat

Ina R. Friedman

Illustrated by Allen Say

In our house, some days we eat with chopsticks
and some days we eat with knives and forks.
For me, it's natural.

When my mother met my father, she was a Japanese schoolgirl and he was an American sailor. His ship was stationed in Yokohama.

Every day, my father, whose name is John, walked in the park with my mother, Aiko. They sat on a bench and talked. But my father was afraid to invite my mother to dinner.

If we go to a restaurant, he thought, I'll go hungry because I don't know how to eat with chopsticks. And if I go hungry, I'll act like a bear. Then Aiko won't like me. I'd better not ask her to dinner.

My mother wondered why my father never invited her to dinner. Perhaps John is afraid I don't know how to eat with a knife and fork and I'll look silly, she thought. Maybe it is best if he doesn't invite me to dinner.

So they walked and talked and never ate a bowl of rice or a piece of bread together.

One day, the captain of my father's ship said, "John, in three weeks the ship is leaving Japan."

My father was sad. He wanted to marry my mother. How can I ask her to marry me? he thought. I don't even know if we like the same food. And if we don't, we'll go hungry. It's hard to be happy if you're hungry. I'll have to find out what food she likes. And I'll have to learn to eat with chopsticks.

So he went to a Japanese restaurant.

Everyone sat on cushions around low tables. My father bowed to the waiter. "Please, teach me to eat with chopsticks."

"Of course," said the waiter, bowing.

The waiter brought a bowl of rice and a plate of sukiyaki. Sukiyaki is made of small pieces of meat, vegetables, and tofu. It smelled good. My father wanted to gobble it up.

The waiter placed two chopsticks between my father's fingers. "Hold the bottom chopstick still. Move the top one to pick up the food," the waiter said.

My father tried, but the meat slipped off his chopstick and fell on his lap.

The waiter came back with a bowl of soup. How can I eat soup with chopsticks? my father thought.

"Drink," said the waiter. "Drink from the bowl."

"Thank goodness," my father said. After the soup my father felt better. He picked up the chopsticks. Finally, my father put one piece of meat in his mouth. Delicious!

"More soup, please," he said.

After three bowls of soup my father felt much better. Then he practiced some more with his chopsticks. Soon, there was more sukiyaki in his belly than on the floor. But it was too late to call my mother. He had to run back to his ship.

That night, my mother was sad. Every other day my father had come to see her. That day he did not come. He did not call on the telephone. Perhaps he was tired of walking and talking. Perhaps he was ashamed of her because she did not know how to eat with a knife and fork. Perhaps his ship had sailed away. All night she could not sleep.

And all night my father sat on his bunk, pretending to pick up sukiyaki.

195

The next morning my father called my mother. "Please, will you eat dinner with me tonight?"

"Yes!" my mother shouted into the phone. First she was happy. Then she was afraid. She took her schoolbooks and ran to the house of Great Uncle.

Great Uncle had visited England. He had seen the British Museum. He had eaten dinners with Englishmen.

My mother knocked at the door. Great Uncle opened it.

"Why are you so sad, child?" he asked.

"Because I must learn to eat with a knife and fork by seven o'clock tonight."

Great Uncle nodded. "Foreign ways are quite strange. Why do you want to eat with a knife and fork?"

My mother blushed.

"Is it the American sailor?" Great Uncle asked. "I see . . . Here, take this note to your teacher. At lunchtime I will come and take you to a foreign restaurant. By seven o'clock tonight you will eat with a knife and fork."

My mother picked up her school bag and bowed.

"No," Great Uncle stuck out his hand. "In the West you shake hands."

197

The restaurant had red carpets and many lights. Great Uncle pulled out a chair for my mother. "In the West, men help ladies into chairs," he told her.

My mother looked at the small fork and the large fork on the left. She looked at the knife, little spoon, and big spoon on the right. Her head grew dizzy.

"Different utensils for different foods," Great Uncle said.

"How strange to dirty so many things," said my mother. "A chopstick is a chopstick. I can eat everything with two chopsticks."

When the waiter brought the soup, Great Uncle pointed at the large spoon. "Dip it slowly, bring it to your mouth. Sip quietly."

My mother's hand trembled. The soup spilled onto the white cloth.

"You'll learn," Great Uncle encouraged her.

When my mother was finished with the soup, the waiter brought her a plate of mashed potatoes, roast beef, and peas.

"This is the way Westerners eat," Great Uncle said. "With the knife and fork they cut the meat. Then they hold the fork upside down in their left hand. Like birds, they build a nest of mashed potatoes. They put the peas in the nest with the knife. Then they slip the nest into their mouth. Try it."

The mashed potatoes were not difficult. But the peas rolled all over the plate. "Impossible," said my mother. "I'll never learn by seven o'clock tonight."

"You can learn anything," Great Uncle said. "Try again. More mashed potatoes and peas, please," he said to the waiter.

At seven o'clock my father came to see my mother.

"Why didn't you wear your kimono?" he asked. "We are going to a Japanese restaurant."

"A Japanese restaurant? Don't you think I know how to eat Western food?" my mother asked.

"Of course. Don't you think I know how to eat Japanese food?"

"Of course."

"Then, tonight we'll eat meat and potatoes. Tomorrow night we'll eat sukiyaki."

"Tomorrow night I will wear my kimono," my mother said. She started to bow. Then she stopped and put out her hand. My father shook it.

My father ordered two plates of mashed potatoes, roast beef, and peas. He watched my mother cut the meat into pieces. He stared when she turned over her fork and made a bird's nest. He was amazed.

"You are very clever with a knife and fork," he said.

"Thank you," said my mother.

"You must teach me," my father said. "That's a new way of eating peas."

"Teach you?"

"Yes, Americans don't eat that way." He slid his fork under some peas and put them in his mouth.

My mother stared at him. "But Great Uncle taught me. He lived in England. He knows the ways of the West."

My father began to laugh. "He taught you to eat like an Englishman. Americans eat differently."

"Oh dear," my mother said. "A chopstick is a chopstick. Everyone uses them in the same way."

"Yes. When we are married we'll eat only with chopsticks." He took her hand.

"Married! If I marry you I want to eat like an American."

"I'll teach you to eat with a knife and fork and you teach me to use chopsticks."

My mother shook my father's hand. My father bowed.

That's why at our house some days we eat with chopsticks and some days we eat with knives and forks.

What can I learn from this story?

People all over the world have **customs.** Customs are special ways people have of doing things. Each country has its own special customs.

Sometimes it is hard to learn other people's customs. Aiko and John had different eating customs. At first they found it hard to eat in a new way.

Today the girl's family eats both ways. Some days they eat with knives and forks. Some days they eat with chopsticks.

Think About This

Why did Aiko and John have such different ways of eating?

Where did John and Aiko live?

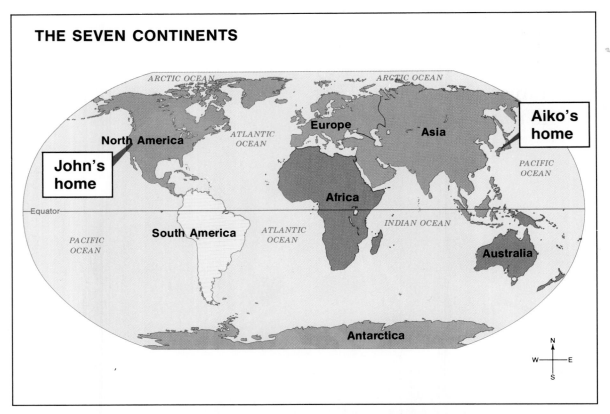

THE SEVEN CONTINENTS

This is a map of the world. It shows the seven **continents** and four oceans. Continents are the largest bodies of land on Earth.

John came from the United States. The United States is on the continent of North America. Find North America on the map.

Aiko came from Japan. Japan is part of the continent of Asia. Find Asia on the map.

What are the names of the other five continents?

Think About This

On what continent do John and Aiko live now?

What do the continents look like?

The story took place in Asia. Asia is the largest continent. The many countries of Asia are very different from one another.

In some parts of northern Asia there are huge plains. It is too cold there to grow many crops.

In southern Asia it is very warm. Some countries get a lot of warm rain. There are beautiful forests in these countries.

Australia is the only continent that is one country. Parts of Australia are plains. Farmers grow crops and raise animals there.

There are also many deserts in Australia. Few people live in the deserts.

Europe is a small continent with many countries.

There are many towns and cities in the countries of Europe. Often towns were built on rivers. Some towns stayed small. Some grew into big cities.

South America is a big continent. It is made up of 13 countries.

This lake is high in the mountains. It is the highest large lake in the world. The weather here is cool all year.

It is always warm in this beautiful city in South America. People can enjoy both the mountains and the beach here.

Africa is a big continent with many countries.

North Africa is hot and dry with deserts. People can live only where they can find water.

Other parts of Africa have plenty of water. Long rivers run through green forests. There are also plains near big cities. You can still see wild animals running on the plains.

Antarctica is the coldest continent. It has ice and snow everywhere. Penguins live there. Very few people live in Antarctica.

Look at the pictures at the top of this page. The first picture shows the Earth. It was taken from space. You can see that the Earth is like a round ball.

The second picture shows a **globe.** The globe is a **model**, or small copy, of the Earth. It is round, too. The blue parts of the globe show water. The other colors show land.

Look at the drawings on page 211. The drawing on the left shows one-half of the globe. The drawing on the right shows the other half.

Look at the drawing on the left and answer the questions.

1. Which three continents can you see?
2. Which oceans can you see?

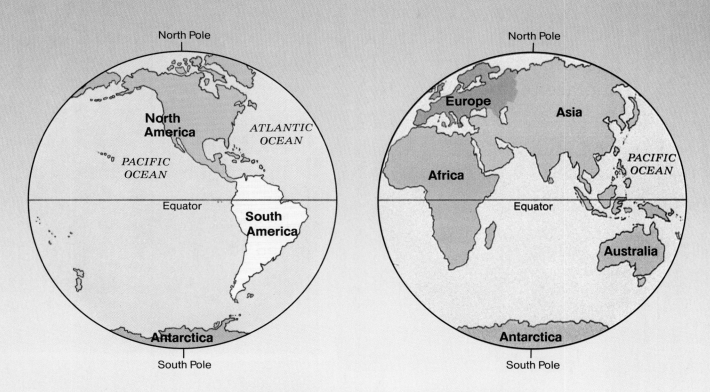

Globes show the **North Pole** and the **South Pole.**
Halfway between the two poles is the **equator,** a
make-believe line that divides the Earth into a northern
half and a southern half. Find the North Pole, the
South Pole, and the equator on the drawings of
the globe above.

Look at the drawing on the right and answer the questions.

1. Which continents are north of the equator?
2. Which continents are south of the equator?

Did Aiko and John live north or south of the equator?

How can I visit people who live in different places?

There are many ways you could go to different places. You could go in an airplane, in a train, or in a ship. Airplanes, trains, and ships are kinds of **transportation.** Transportation is any way of moving people from one place to another.

What kind of transportation do you think Aiko and John used to go from Japan to the United States?

When might John and Aiko have taken a train? This bullet train in Japan is one of the fastest trains in the world.

People use transportation to go places in their own cities and towns. People use cars and bicycles to get to other neighborhoods.

In most cities and towns, buses can take you where you want to go.

Some big cities have subways. Subways are trains that run underground.

Think About This

How do people move goods from one place to another?

How can I talk to people who are far away?

People need to talk to other people. People write letters to other people. Talking and writing to other people is called **communication.**

Sometimes you may talk to neighbors. Sometimes you may talk to people who are far away.

Think About This

Why was communication a problem for Aiko and John?

Some ways you communicate have been used for a long time.

Some other kinds of communication are very new.

PEOPLE
to Know
About

Alexander Graham Bell and His Talking Machine

Alexander Graham Bell taught children who had trouble hearing.

"How do people hear?" he wondered. "How do people talk?" The more he thought about it, the more interested he became in communication.

Alexander thought about inventing a better telegraph. At that time, the telegraph was a way people "talked" over long distances. The telegraph carried electric signals along wires. The signals stood for letters that made up words.

One day Alexander was working with his helper, Thomas A. Watson. They were working on their new telegraph invention. The two men were in different parts of the building. Suddenly, Thomas heard a voice coming from the invention.

"Watson—Come here —I want to see you," he heard Alexander's voice say.

Alexander Graham Bell had made his voice travel over the electric wires. He invented the telephone and changed communication forever.

How do Americans share their customs?

Americans from different countries have their own holidays and celebrations. They celebrate with special customs. Many Americans share their special customs and celebrations with other people.

Think About This

When does your community have parades? What do the parades celebrate?

PLACES to Know About

The Chew Kee Store

The Chew Kee Store is in Fiddletown, California. The store was built by a man who came to California from China. It was built almost 150 years ago.

A few years ago, people decided to save the old store. They decided to fix it and make it look the way it looked when it was new.

They have put many things to see inside the store. There are things to see about California history. There are things about the Chinese people who came to California long ago.

Think About This

Why should anyone want to save the Chew Kee Store?

How are people from all countries alike?

People from all over the world like to dance and sing. Each country has its own songs and dances. These special songs and dances are called folk songs and folk dances. The music for these songs and dances is called folk music.

People wear special costumes for folk dancing. Sometimes they play special musical instruments.

Many people in the United States enjoy the folk songs and folk dances from different countries.

Review

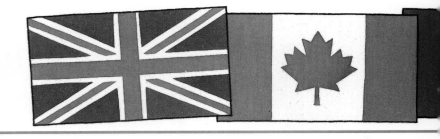

Use New Words

1. Name one **custom** your family has about food.
2. On which **continent** were your parents born?
3. What is a **globe** a **model** of ?
4. Name two kinds of **transportation** that John and Aiko could have used to cross the Pacific Ocean.
5. How did Alexander Graham Bell help **communication**?

Use New Ideas

6. Why is it fun to learn about different customs?
7. How are the seven continents alike?
   How are they different?
8. How do you think transportation will change in the future?

Think About What You Know

Which of these words have to do with communication and which with transportation?

radio   space shuttle   videotape
roller skates   words   horse and wagon

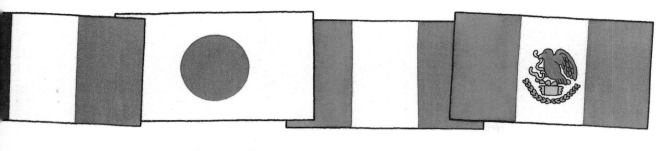

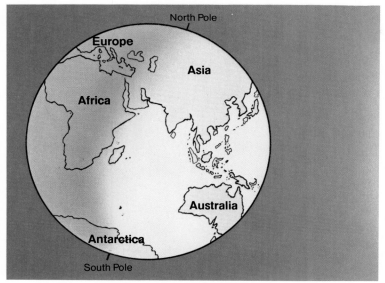

Use New Skills

Look at the picture and answer the questions.

9. Does the picture show a map or a globe?
10. Is Europe north or south of Africa?
11. Is Australia east or west of Africa?
12. Which is closer to Asia, the North Pole or the South Pole?
13. Where does the equator go on the picture?
14. Why can you not find North America on the picture?

Something to Do

Read a story that takes place on another continent. Ask your teacher to help you find a story.

ATLAS

CANADA

Seattle
Olympia ⭐
WASHINGTON

Portland
⭐ Salem
OREGON

NORTH DAKOTA
⭐ Bismarck

Helena ⭐
MONTANA

Billings

IDAHO
⭐ Boise

Pocatello

Pierre ⭐
SOUTH DAKOTA

WYOMING

Casper

Sacramento ⭐
⭐ Carson City

Salt Lake City ⭐
Provo

Cheyenne ⭐

NEBRASKA

NEVADA

UTAH

Denver ⭐
COLORADO
Colorado Springs

KANSAS

CALIFORNIA

Wichita

Las Vegas

OKLAHOMA

PACIFIC OCEAN

Los Angeles

ARIZONA

Santa Fe ⭐
Albuquerque

Oklahoma City

Phoenix ⭐

NEW MEXICO

Tucson

TEXAS

ARCTIC OCEAN

Austin ⭐

MEXICO

ALASKA

CANADA

PACIFIC OCEAN

Anchorage

Kauai

Oahu   HAWAII
Honolulu ⭐

Juneau ⭐

0   250   500   Miles
0   250   500   750 Kilometers

Maui

0   100   200   Miles
0   100 200 300 Kilometers

Hawaii

PACIFIC OCEAN

UNITED STATES OF AMERICA

CANADA

ATLANTIC OCEAN

Gulf of Mexico

BAHAMAS

CUBA

MINNESOTA
Minneapolis • • St. Paul
ux Falls

WISCONSIN
Milwaukee •
Madison ✪

MICHIGAN
Lansing ✪
Detroit •

MAINE
Augusta ✪
Portland •

Burlington •
Montpelier ✪
VERMONT
NEW HAMPSHIRE
Concord ✪
Manchester •
Boston •

NEW YORK
Albany ✪
Springfield • Providence ✪
Hartford ✪
MASSACHUSETTS
RHODE ISLAND
CONNECTICUT
Bridgeport •

IOWA
Cedar Rapids •
Des Moines ✪
Omaha •
incoln

Chicago •

Fort Wayne •
INDIANA
Indianapolis ✪

OHIO
Columbus ✪
Cleveland •

PENNSYLVANIA
Harrisburg ✪
Philadelphia •

Newark •
• New York City
Trenton ✪
NEW JERSEY
Dover ✪
DELAWARE

ILLINOIS
Springfield ✪

Baltimore •
Washington D.C. ✪
Annapolis ✪
MARYLAND

WEST VIRGINIA
Huntington •
Charleston ✪

VIRGINIA
Richmond ✪
Norfolk •

Topeka •
Jefferson City ✪
St. Louis •
MISSOURI

Louisville •
Frankfort •
KENTUCKY

NORTH CAROLINA
Raleigh ✪
Charlotte •

Tulsa •
Nashville ✪
TENNESSEE

ARKANSAS
Fort Smith •
Little Rock ✪
Memphis •

Columbia •
SOUTH CAROLINA
Charleston •

Atlanta ✪
Birmingham •
GEORGIA

MISSISSIPPI
ALABAMA
Montgomery ✪
Columbus •

Jackson ✪

LOUISIANA
Tallahassee ✪
Jacksonville •

Baton Rouge ✪
Biloxi •
New Orleans
Houston •

FLORIDA

MAP KEY
──── National boundary
──── State boundary
✪ National capital
✪ State capital
• Large city

N
W E
S

0	100	200	300 Miles
0	100	200	300	400 Kilometers

223

ATLAS

National boundary

ALB. Albania
AUST. Austria
C. AF. REP. Central African Republic
CZECH. Czechoslovakia
E. GER. East Germany
HUNG. Hungary
NETH. Netherlands
SWITZ. Switzerland
U. ARAB EMIR. United Arab Emirates
W. GER. West Germany
YEMEN (P.D.R.) People's Democratic
  Republic of Yemen
YUGO. Yugoslavia

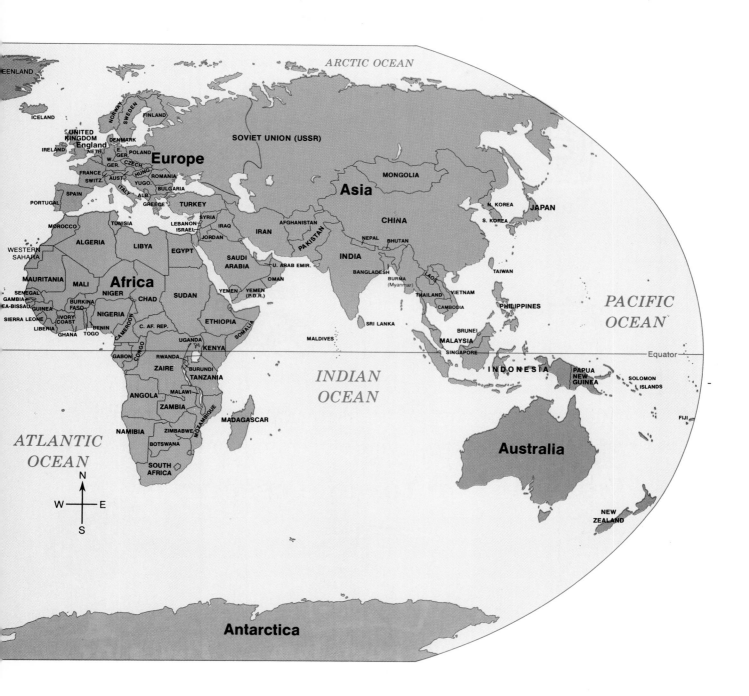

ARCTIC OCEAN

EENLAND

ICELAND

NORWAY
SWEDEN
FINLAND

SOVIET UNION (USSR)

UNITED
KINGDOM
IRELAND
England
DENMARK
NETH.
E.
GER.
POLAND
W.
GER.
CZECH.
Europe
HUNG.
ROMANIA
FRANCE
SWITZ.
AUST.
YUGO.
BULGARIA
SPAIN
ITALY
ALB.
GREECE
TURKEY
PORTUGAL

MONGOLIA

Asia

N. KOREA
JAPAN
S. KOREA

CHINA

MOROCCO
TUNISIA
LEBANON
ISRAEL
SYRIA
IRAQ
JORDAN
IRAN
AFGHANISTAN
PAKISTAN
NEPAL
BHUTAN

ALGERIA
LIBYA
EGYPT
INDIA

WESTERN
SAHARA
SAUDI
ARABIA
U. ARAB EMIR.
OMAN
BANGLADESH
BURMA
(Myanmar)
TAIWAN

MAURITANIA
MALI
Africa
NIGER
CHAD
SUDAN
YEMEN
YEMEN
(P.D.R.)
LAOS

SENEGAL
GAMBIA
EA-BISSAU
GUINEA
BURKINA
FASO
THAILAND
VIETNAM
**PACIFIC
OCEAN**
SIERRA LEONE
IVORY
COAST
NIGERIA
CAMEROON
C. AF. REP.
ETHIOPIA
CAMBODIA
PHILIPPINES
LIBERIA
GHANA
TOGO
BENIN
SRI LANKA
BRUNEI
UGANDA
SOMALIA
MALDIVES
MALAYSIA
GABON
CONGO
RWANDA
KENYA
SINGAPORE
Equator
ZAIRE
BURUNDI
TANZANIA
INDONESIA
PAPUA
NEW
GUINEA
SOLOMON
ISLANDS
ANGOLA
MALAWI
ZAMBIA
MOZAMBIQUE
MADAGASCAR
FIJI
**ATLANTIC
OCEAN**
NAMIBIA
ZIMBABWE
BOTSWANA
Australia
SOUTH
AFRICA

*INDIAN
OCEAN*

N
W E
S

NEW
ZEALAND

Antarctica

You Can Make
How You Can Help

Ways for you to save energy

Turn off the lights when you leave the room.

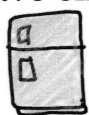

Don't keep the refrigerator door open too long.

Turn off the TV when you are not watching it.

Ride your bike or walk instead of asking for someone to drive you places in a car.

Ways for you to save resources

Shut off water while brushing your teeth.

Reuse paper. Turn sheets over and use the other side. Use paper bags over.

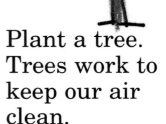

Plant a tree. Trees work to keep our air clean.

A Difference
The Environment

Ways for you to recycle

Never throw something away until you ask "Could this be used again in another way?"

Make a pencil holder from a can.

Make a tree swing from a tire.

Grow plants in a plastic bottle.

Ways to keep our Earth clean

Collect cans to recycle.

Bundle newspapers to recycle.

Wherever you go—pick up litter.

You cannot save the Earth by yourself.
Tell others how to help.
Everyone must work together.

GLOSSARY

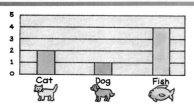

bar graph (p. 114)
A picture that shows how much or how many.

barter (p. 109)
Another word for trade.

capital (p. 144)
The city where laws are made for a state or country.

Capitol Building (p. 144)
The building where Congress meets.

change (p. 23)
To make different or to become different.

city hall (p. 143)
Place where the city's laws are made.

colonies (p. 67)
Communities owned by a faraway country.

communication (p. 214)
Talking and writing to other people.

community (p. 23)
A group of different neighborhoods.

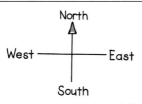

compass rose (p. 36)
A symbol showing the directions on a map.

Congress (p. 144)
Leaders who make the United States' laws.

continents (p. 206)
The seven largest bodies of land on Earth.

crops (p. 60)
Plants farmers grow for food and other things.

custom (p. 205)
A special way you do things.

desert (p. 174)
A dry place where very little rain falls.

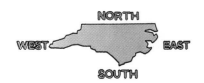

directions (p. 36)
North, south, east, and west are directions.

distance (p. 38)
How far one place is from another.

distance scale (p. 39)
A line on a map that helps you tell how far apart places are.

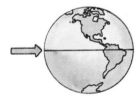

equator (p. 211)
A make-believe line on globes and some maps.

explorers (p. 70)
People who go ahead of others into new lands.

flag (p. 68)
Something every country has. Ours is red, white, and blue.

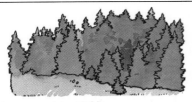

forest (p. 174)
A place where many trees grow.

freedom (p. 68)
What America won in the war with England.

globe (p. 210)
A model of the Earth.

goods (p. 106)
Things that people make or grow.

government (p. 143)
A group of people who make and carry out laws.

group (p. 120)
A number of people together.

history (p. 44)
The way things happened in the past.

income (p. 105)
Money earned by working.

lake (p. 175)
A body of water with land all around it.

laws (p. 141)
Rules that everyone must obey.

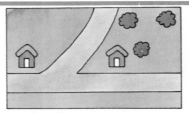

map (p. 1)
A picture of a place.

map key (p. 1)
A list of symbols used on a map.

mayor (p. 143)
A city's most important leader.

model (p. 210)
A small copy of something.

needs (p. 95)
Things we cannot live without.

neighborhood (p. 6)
A place where people live and work.

neighbors (p. 28)
People who live near each other.

North Pole (p. 211)
The farthest north you can go on the Earth.

ocean (p. 175)
A very large body of salt water.

plain (p. 174)
A place where the land is very flat.

President (p. 69)
The leader of the United States.

river (p. 175)
A stream that carries water to lakes or oceans.

rule (p. 140)
What you may or may not do.

save (p. 110)
To keep for later use.

service (p. 107)
Something someone does for others.

settlers (p. 65)
People who moved to new lands.

South Pole (p. 211)
The farthest south you can go on the Earth.

state (p. 154)
One of the 50 parts of the United States.

suburb (p. 24)
A community near a city.

symbol (p. 1)
A drawing that stands for something real.

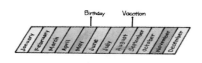

timeline (p. 72)
A line marked to show in what order things happened.

transportation (p. 212)
Any way of moving people or things from place to place.

volunteers (p. 111)
People who work for free.

vote (p. 137)
How some groups choose their leaders or decide things.

wants (p. 104)
Things people would like to have.

INDEX

Key: (t), top; (b), bottom; (l), left; (r), right; (c), center.

Photographs

Front Cover (t), Robert Frerck/Odyssey Productions; Front Cover(b), Wilton S. Tifft; Title page, Robert Frerck/Odyssey Productions; Back Cover, Wilton S. Tifft.

Table of contents: iii(t), Roy Morsch/The Stock Market; iii(b), The Bettmann Archive; iv(t), Pete Saloutos/TSW/After-Image; iv(b), Terry Donnelly/Tom Stack & Assoc.; v, David Falconer/West Stock.

UNIT 1: 4–5, HBJ Photo/Julie Fletcher; 6(t), HBJ Photo/Beverly Brosius; 6(b), HBJ Photo/Gary Slack; 23(t), HBJ Photo/Beverly Brosius; 23(b), Dana Knight/Picturesque; 24, J. McWee/FPG; 28(t), HBJ Photo/Beverly Brosius; 28(b), HBJ Photo; 30(t), Susanna Pashko/Envision; 30(b), Roy Morsch/The Stock Market; 31, Roy Morsch/The Stock Market; 32, Cleveland Public Library; 34(t), HBJ Photo/Beverly Brosius; 34(c), Suzanne J. Engelmann/SuperStock; 34(b), Steve Elmore/Tom Stack & Assoc.; 35(tl), Lew Merrim/Monkmeyer Press; 35(tr), Grant LeDuc/Monkmeyer Press; 35(bl), Dan McCoy/Rainbow; 35(br), R. M. Collins III/The Image Works.

UNIT 2: 42–43, John Neubauer; 44(t), HBJ Photo/Beverly Brosius; 44(c), HBJ Photo/Terry Sinclair; 44(b), HBJ Photo/C. Bruce Forester; 58, HBJ Photo/Beverly Brosius; 59(t), HBJ Photo/Beverly Brosius; 59(b), Historical Picture Service; 60(t), Metropolitan Museum of Art, Rogers Fund, 1907, THE ROCKY MOUNTAINS, Albert Bierstadt; 60(b), The Royal Ontario Museum, Toronto, Canada, detail from THE FALLS AT COLVILLE; 61, HBJ Photo/Beverly Brosius; 64, HBJ Photo/Beverly Brosius; 67(l), from the collections of The Louisiana State Museum, "Olivier Plantation"; 67(r), Peabody Museum of Salem, photo by Mark Sexton, "Appleton's Wharf"; 68, HBJ Photo/Rick Der; 69, Art Collection of the Union League of Philadelphia; 70, HBJ Photo/Beverly Brosius; 71, The Bettmann Archive.

UNIT 3: 76–77, Robert Frerck/Odyssey Productions; 78(t), HBJ Photo/Beverly Brosius; 78(b), Brown Brothers; 95(t), HBJ Photo/Beverly Brosius; 95(b), HBJ Photo/Earl Kogler; 96(t), HBJ Photo/Beverly Brosius; 96(b), HBJ Photo/Karen Rantzman; 97(tl), HBJ Photo/Karen Rantzman; 97(tr), HBJ Photo/Elliott Varner Smith; 97(br), HBJ Photo/Alec Duncan; 98(t), Ross/FPG; 98(b), HBJ Photo/Erik Arnesen; 100(t), HBJ Photo/Beverly Brosius; 100(cl), HBJ Photo; 100(cr), The National Cotton Council of America; 100(b), U.S.D.A.; 101(tl), HBJ Photo/Alec Duncan, courtesy of Levi Strauss & Company; 101(tr), HBJ Photo/Alec Duncan, courtesy of Levi Strauss & Company; 101(bl), HBJ Photo/Rodney Jones; 101(br), HBJ Photo/Rodney Jones; 102, The Granger Collection; 103(l), HBJ Photo/Dover Publications; 103(r), HBJ Photo/Dover Publications; 104(t), HBJ Photo/Beverly Brosius; 104(bl), HBJ Photo/Karen Rantzman; 104(br), HBJ Photo/Rodney Jones; 105(t), HBJ Photo/Beverly Brosius; 105(cl), HBJ Photo/Karen Rantzman; 105(cr), HBJ Photo/Karen Rantzman; 105(bl), HBJ Photo/Karen Rantzman; 105(br), HBJ Photo/Erik Arnesen; 106(tl), HBJ Photo; 106(bl), John Colwell/Grant Heilman Photography; 106(br), HBJ Photo; 107(tl), HBJ Photo/Elliott Varner Smith; 107(tr), D. C. Lowe/The Stock Shop; 107(b), HBJ Photo/Alec Duncan; 108(t), HBJ Photo/Beverly Brosius; 108(c), Milt & Joan Mann/Cameramann International; 108(b), Pawel Kanicki/Transglobe; 109(t), Steve Vidler/Leo de Wys, Inc.; 109(b), Christiana Dittmann/Rainbow; 110(t), HBJ Photo/Beverly Brosius; 110(bl), HBJ Photo/Alec Duncan; 110(br), HBJ Photo/Rodney Jones; 111(t), HBJ Photo/Beverly Brosius; 111(cl), HBJ Photo/Karen Rantzman; 111(cr), HBJ Photo/Karen Rantzman; 111(bl), HBJ Photo; 111(br), HBJ Photo; 112(l), HBJ Photo; 113, Jeane Stilwell/Orlando All Children's Playground.

UNIT 4: 118–119, HBJ Photo/Earl Kogler; 120(t), HBJ Photo/Beverly Brosius; 120(c), C. M. Rothwell/FPG; 120(b), Don Klumpp/The Image Bank; 137(t), HBJ Photo/Beverly Brosius; 137(b), Mark Richards; 138(l), SuperStock; 138(r), Steve Elmore; 139(t), Keith Glasgow; 139(b), Pete Saloutos/TSW/After-Image; 140(t), HBJ Photo/Beverly Brosius; 140(cl), HBJ Photo/Karen Rantzman; 140(cr), Keith Glasgow; 140(bl), HBJ Photo/Karen Rantzman; 140(br), Gabe Palmer/TSW/After-Image; 141(t), HBJ Photo/Beverly Brosius; 141(cl), Carol Kitman; 141(cr), HBJ Photo/Karen Rantzman; 141(bl), Philip Jon Bailey/The Picture Cube; 141(br), Mary Kate Denny/PhotoEdit; 142(t), Bob Daemmrich; 142(b), Neena M. Wilmot; 143(t), HBJ Photo/Beverly Brosius; 143(b), HBJ Photo/Karen Rantzman; 144(t), Rick Maiman/Sygma; 144(bl), Everett C. Johnson/TSW/After-Image; 144(br), David Valdez/The White House; 145(tl), HBJ Photo/Beverly Brosius; 145(tr), John Neubauer/PhotoEdit; 145(b), Supreme Court Historical Society; 146(tl), HBJ Photo/Karen Rantzman; 146(tc), HBJ Photo/Norman Prince; 146(tr), HBJ Photo/Rick Der; 146(bl), HBJ Photo/Karen Rantzman; 146(bc), HBJ Photo/Richard Reeves; 146(br), HBJ Photo/Rick Der; 147(t), HBJ Photo/Erik Arnesen; 147(ct), HBJ Photo/Rick Der; 147(cl), HBJ Photo/Karen Rantzman; 147(cr), HBJ Photo/Karen Rantzman; 147(bl), HBJ Photo/Rick Der; 147(br), HBJ Photo/Karen Rantzman; 148(t), HBJ Photo/Beverly Brosius; 148(bl), Joseph Devenney/The Image Bank; 148(bcl), Daniel MacDonald/The Stock Shop; 148(bcr), H. Mark Weidman; 148(br), Dan Peha; 149, British Information Services.

UNIT 5: 152–153, Rick Godin; 154, HBJ Photo/Beverly Brosius; 156–170(all), HBJ Photo; 171(t), HBJ Photo/Beverly Brosius; 171(b), Audrey Gibson; 172, HBJ Photo/Beverly Brosius; 174(t), HBJ Photo/Beverly Brosius; 174(ct), Tom Dietrich/TSW; 174(cb), Craig Aurness/Woodfin Camp & Assoc.; 174(b), Terry Donnelly/Tom Stack & Assoc.; 175(t), Dale Jorgenson/Tom Stack & Assoc.; 175(c), Earl Scott/Photo Researchers; 176, copyright © 1983, Grandma Moses Properties Co., New York; 177, Ifor Thomas/copyright © 1973, Grandma Moses Properties Co., New York, "White House Collection".; 180(t), HBJ Photo/Beverly Brosius; 180(bl), Richard Steedman/The Stock Market; 180(br), R. Krubner/H. Armstrong Roberts; 181(tr), E. E. Otto/FPG; 182(t), HBJ Photo/Beverly Brosius; 182(b), Jim Brandenburg/Frozen Images; 183(t), National Film Board of Canada; 183(b), Porterfield/Chickering.

UNIT 6: 186–187, Steve Vidler/Leo de Wys, Inc.; 188(t), HBJ Photo/Beverly Brosius; 188(b), Owen Franken/Stock, Boston; 205(t), HBJ Photo/Beverly Brosius; 205(b), Cameramann/The Image Works; 207(t), HBJ Photo/Beverly Brosius; 207(b), F. Prenzel/Photri; 208(t), Atoz Images/TSW; 208(c), Steve Vidler/TSW/After-Image; 208(b), Foto Messerschmidt/FPG; 209(b), R. Harrington/FPG; 210(l), NASA; 210(r), HBJ Photo/Karen Rantzman; 212(t), HBJ Photo/Beverly Brosius; 212(c), Milt & Joan Mann/Cameramann International; 212(b), Dallas & John Heaton/TSW/After-Image; 213(t), HBJ Photo/Karen Rantzman; 213(b), Tony Mooman/UMI Photo; 214(t), HBJ Photo/Beverly Brosius; 214(bl), HBJ Photo/Earl Kogler; 214(br), V. Beller-Smith; 215(t), HBJ Photo/Earl Kogler; 215(b), NASA; 216, The Granger Collection; 217(t), Milt & Joan Mann/Cameramann International; 217(cr), David Falconer/West Stock; 217(b), Robert Frerck/Odyssey Productions; 218(l), Daniel D'Agostini; 218(r), Daniel D'Agostini; 219(t), HBJ Photo/Beverly Brosius; 219(c), Samelius/H. Armstrong Roberts; 219(b), Milt & Joan Mann/Cameramann International.

Illustrations N.M. Bodecker: 7–22. Barbara Cooney: 79–94. Rosemary Deasey: 115, 151. Walter Gasper: 114, 117. Terry Hoff: 59, 60, 64, 65, 66. Intergraphics: 22, 37, 38, 39, 41, 66, 221M. Michael Latoria: 155–170. Steve Parton and Allan Davis: 45–57. PC&F: 4, 5, 25–27, 29, 32, 33, 40–43, 61, 70, 73–77, 96, 102, 103, 115–119, 150–154, 184–187, 216, 220, 221t, 221b. Allen Say: 189–204. Sally Schaedler: 121–136.

Maps R.R. Donnelley Cartographic Services: 172, 173, 177, 185, 211.